Win at the
CASINO

FULLY REVISED

Win at the
CASINO

Play the Odds
Play it Smart

Dennis R.
Harrison

Lifetime Books, Inc.
Hollywood, Florida

Copyright © 1996 by Dennis R. Harrison

ISBN 0-8119-0837-2

All rights reserved. Published by Lifetime Books, Inc., 2131 Hollywood Blvd., Holly-wood, FL 33020.

This publication is designed to provide accurate and authoritative information in re-gard to the subject matter covered. It is sold with the understanding that the publisher is not engaged in rendering legal, accounting, or other professional service. If legal advice or other assistance is required, the services of a competent professional person should be sought. *From A Declaration of Principles jointly adopted by a Committee of the American Bar Association and a Committee of Publishers.*

Library of Congress Cataloging-in-Publication Data

Harrison, Dennis R.
    Win at the casino : play the odds, play it smart / by Dennis R. Harrison. -- Fully rev.
        p. cm.
    Includes bibliographical references.
    ISBN 0-8119-0837-2 (alk. paper)
    1. Gambling. 2. Casinos. I. Title.
GV1301.H28   1996
795-- dc20   96-5077
                                                               CIP

Printed in Canada

Contents

 # Introduction

If you are one of those people who do not care whether you win or lose at the casino of your choice, you do not need to read this book. If you are a professional gambler, you do not need to read this book. If you have a need or a psychological compulsion to lose money, you do not need to read this book. If you enjoy the idea of giving your money to the casinos, of making a willful donation in exchange for a few free drinks and a "good" time, reading this book is a genuine waste of your time.

However, if you would like to be one of the lucky few who actually win money, reading this book can help. I cannot guarantee you will beat the casinos at every turn of the cards, every roll of the dice, or every spin of the wheel. But, if you listen to what I have to say and apply a few of my general principles, you will reduce your losses and begin the arduous journey leading to consistent success.

This book covers the major games offered in casinos: Blackjack, Craps, Roulette, Baccarat, Keno, Slot Machines, Sports Book Wagering and Casino Style Poker. In addition, this new revised edition also covers several new games which have proved attractive to us gamblers: Pai Gow Poker, Let It Ride, and Caribbean Stud. But before we can discuss these games, we must first consider a few ideas which can help you enormously.

First, I would like to talk about attitude. No, I'm not going to suggest that you enroll in a Dale Carnegie course. Neither am I promoting Norman Vincent Peale or any other author who claims that you can change your life with the proper attitude. But consider for a moment what took place when you decided to visit Las Vegas, Reno, Atlantic City or your new local casino. You called your friendly travel agent to arrange the three day/two night venture and paid in advance. You found a neighbor to feed the pets, perhaps convinced a few friends or relatives to join you. Then, before you left your home town, you engaged in a small amount of soul searching and decided how much money you could afford to lose. Am I right?

Perhaps you decided on a few hundred, maybe it was several thousand. The amount makes no difference. For the purpose of my point we will assume you decided on $1,000. You determined that losing a thousand dollars would not "kill" you. Your rationale was simple: Even if you lost the whole thousand you would still be able to pay the bills when you returned home, your investments would not be affected, and the $1,000 was really just "fun" money, anyway.

I'm not saying you did anything wrong. You merely experienced the same thought process as millions of other people and reached pretty much the same conclusions. But think about it for a moment. Your first assumption regarding the trip was that you were going to *lose* money. Now, I ask you, how far would you have gotten with your life if you had always assumed that you would lose?

And why did you make the "losing" assumption in the first place? The reasons are numerous, here are a few:

** You've heard of all the various games of chance, but you don't really understand them, so how could you possibly expect to win?
** People always lose. The gambling/casino business is prospering because *everybody* loses.
** Only "lucky" people ever win anything, and you most certainly have never been lucky.
** The people you know who claim they won money always tend to exaggerate, so you have never really believed their preposterous stories.

Believe me, if you thought of any of these reasons, you are not alone. Nearly every person I've interviewed assumed that he or she would lose money. And nearly all of those people were correct. Nearly all of them did, in fact, lose money.

But what happens when you *don't* expect to lose? What happens when you actually, God forbid, expect to win? Will you return home with all that money you brought plus some extra? Maybe.

I am not saying a change of attitude will make you a winner. But a change of attitude can help. And when coupled with other basic truths contained in this book, a better attitude will assist you in becoming a winner.

Assuming you will lose your $1,000 is not the way to start your trip. Do you really want to lose that grand? Of course not. Do the casinos want to take it? Absolutely not. Surprised? You shouldn't be. Think about it. The casinos do not want you returning to Iowa or New York, Idaho or Calgary without any money. They really don't want to bleed you dry. If you lose your entire gambling stake, you may never come back to gamble again, and that's bad for business. The casinos would prefer that you lose money, but not all of it, not even a majority of it. They would like you to lose half, or a quarter, or even ten per cent, but not all of it.

In point of fact, the perfect scenario for the casinos would be something like this: You arrive late Friday afternoon to begin your holiday fling. You brought $1,000 for gambling. You check into your hotel, gamble until two o'clock in the morning, and lose $350 testing your luck at a potpourri of Roulette, Slots, Craps and Blackjack. Saturday you lose another $80. Saturday night, after the dinner show, you drop another $280 at the Crap tables before deciding you're a born loser. It takes all the courage you can muster to avoid severe depression, because you now have only $290 out of the $1,000 you started with and your plane does not leave until three o'clock Sunday afternoon. It's decision time. Do you risk the balance of your gambling fund in an attempt to recoup your losses? Or do you play Keno for a dollar a game to while away the remaining hours of your stay?

Your thought process goes like this: Damnit, I came here expecting to lose $1,000. So far I've only lost $710. What the hell? It's only money. Some people bet more than $290 on one hand of Blackjack. I might as well go for broke.

You can't sleep very well Saturday night, so you're up at sunrise. After a quick breakfast, a return to the Crap tables puts $60 winnings into your pockets. A whirl at Roulette proves fruitful when your favorite number comes up on your very last bet. You then win another $160, lose back part of it, but have the presence of mind to walk away from the spinning wheel with $100 of the Casino's money. A try at Blackjack proves frustrating as you can do no better than break even. But another stop at a Crap game nets you another $130. Now, instead of only $290, you have $580 and you're positively convinced your luck has changed. Unfortunately, a glance at your watch discloses that your bus to the airport leaves in ten minutes. You don't want to leave yet. So, even though you risk missing the bus, you pause at the exit doors to transfer three quarters from you pocket into a slot machine. The result? You hit a $300 payoff and leave town with $880.

You're elated because you "won" $590 on the last day of your stay. You can't wait to come back again. The casino is happy, too, since you'll probably return someday to lose another $120. The major casinos have millions of visitors each year. Even if each visitor only loses $120...well, the totals are staggering. In 1993, there were approximately 25 million visitors to Las Vegas. What do you get when you multiply 25 million times a hundred and twenty dollars? The answer looks like this: $3,000,000,000.

Now the critical question: Were you a winner or a loser? If your answer is a loser, you're not being completely honest with yourself. Sure, you brought $1,000 and left town with only $880. Yes, you actually lost $120. But what did you tell your friends when you got home? Probably something like this: "I had a bad streak when I first got there, but I won like crazy on the last day. I only wish I could have stayed a few more days. How did I do, overall? Oh, I think I finished about even. And I hit a $300 jackpot on the slot machines!"

Did you lie? Of course not. You're happy because you avoided losing all your money, and you did win on your last day.

What I have just described may be a perfect scenario for the casinos, but it is not a good one for you. For, on your next visit, you are not going to lose any money. And if you thought you had a good time even when you lost a little, think about what a good time you'll have if you win.

So your first step is to assume you can win. Then what?

Here comes the hard part. In order to actually win, you must take the time to learn something about the games you're going to play. You must avoid the stupid bets, stay away from the games where the odds are stacked against you, and sidestep the awaiting pitfalls. You must understand the chances of success or failure at each game and plan accordingly. Is that reasonable? Yes! Is that intelligent? Of course!

Now you're making progress. You're going to assume that you can win and you're going to learn the games. However, a good attitude and a little knowledge of each game will do nothing more than get you into trouble. The old adage about a little knowledge being dangerous is particularly true with gambling. What you really need is *in-depth* knowledge of all the games.

But this raises another question. Is it reasonable to believe that you can become "expert" in all the games? No. Can you become expert in one? Yes! You may prefer Craps or Roulette, Baccarat or Blackjack. Whichever your choice, it does not matter. The point is that you must study your choice. This book will teach you the basics of all the major games and either give you tips on how to win or tips on how not to lose. After reading this book you still might lose, but you won't lose as much as most people, and you'll be able to avoid disaster. But you must choose one of the games as your specialty.

My forte is Blackjack. I've studied it extensively, I play it with the confidence that stems from knowledge and experience. I have lost money playing Blackjack on only two occasions. I lost money on my very first visit to Las Vegas, a trip made at a time when I had no knowledge of the game; I also lost at another time when I was trying to impress a few relatives with my expertise. But, excluding those two occasions, I have never lost money playing Blackjack. Yes, I have played more than twice. Am I lucky? No, not particularly, no more so than you. And if my statement about never losing sounds too ludicrous to accept, let me explain.

I normally visit the various gambling Meccas for two to five days at a time. During these vacations, I have lost money at Blackjack for an hour, for a day, and even for several days. I have lost for one day, won for three; I have lost for three days, won for one. One time I lost for an incredible ninety hours and only won for six, but I still left town with winnings instead of losses. On various trips I have won as little as three and a half dollars, as much as several thousand dollars. To me, the amount I win has little importance. The key point, in my mind, is that winning money is vastly preferable to losing it. And, the reason that I win is that I *know* how to play Blackjack.

Okay. You select the game of your choice. Now, yet another question presents itself. Is it reasonable to assume that you will play *only* your specialty, to the exclusion of all the other games, for your entire trip? Can you avoid the temptation to pop a few coins in a slot machine, control the urge to wager on your favorite number at Roulette? Can you ignore those joyful cries emanating from the Crap tables? I doubt it. Even if you know that you'll lose, you'll still want to test your luck. But it is *how* you play the games that will determine whether you leave town with winnings of losses.

A winning attitude and in-depth knowledge of your specialty must be combined with rational, intelligent money management. Here's what I suggest: After you determine the size of your gambling fund, divide it into two groups. Group A should be at least eighty percent of the fund, to be used only on the game that you have mastered. Group B, the other twenty percent or less, can then be used to experiment with the other games, to test your luck, or to help pass time between your serious gambling sessions. In other words, plan on playing seriously with at least eighty percent of your funds and using the rest on whatever strikes your fancy. And under no circumstances should you ever use any of your serious money to supplement the loss of fun money. Once the fun money is gone, it is gone, so use it sparingly.

If your gambling fund is $1000, you would gamble with $800, toy with $200. Who knows what may happen? Perhaps while playing with your fun money you'll win a jackpot at the slot machines or hit your lucky number five times in succession at Roulette. If that happens, great! But don't count on it.

Remember this: The casinos win the majority of their money from players who do not have the slightest idea of what they are doing. And they win the rest of their money because the odds are stacked so badly against the players that it is almost impossible to win. Consequently, you must do three things before you can start on the road to success.

1). You must assume that you will win. 2). You must master the game of your choice. 3). You must have a money management system, and you must stick to that system, no matter what happens.

If you can take these three simple steps, you will be better off than ninety percent of the people whom you see in Las Vegas or any of the other gambling meccas. You can join the elite club of people who consistently win money.

Now, a word of caution. Strange things happen to perfectly reasonable human beings when they walk into a casino. The man who won't bet more than ten cents back home at the local monthly poker club is seized by a fit of frenzy and finds himself betting $25 on a single hand of Blackjack. The grandmother from Iowa who thought gambling was the "devil's handiwork" drops $300 playing the nickel slot machines. The person who normally follows a religious routine of rest and exercise sits at a Roulette table for 94 consecutive hours. People become obsessed and possessed. Don't let it happen to you.

Take frequent breaks from the action. Use those lavish swimming pools the hotels built for your use. Enjoy a short nap each afternoon. Go to the lounge shows. In short, do anything to take your mind off gambling. No one can gamble intelligently for long time periods. Do your gambling in sessions lasting no more than an hour or two. This is just as essential as the three steps we discussed earlier.

Good luck and good reading.

Post Script:

The original version of this book was written in 1980. Back then, if you wanted to visit a casino your choices were pretty much limited to either Atlantic City or several destinations in Nevada. Now, in 1996, you can visit a casino in darn near every state in the country, whether it be on dry land, a riverboat or an Indian Reservation. The explosive growth of the casino gambling industry has been nothing short of phenomenal. Of course, in most cases, new casinos were built so that local governments could add billions of additional dollars in tax revenue. Yet, the bottom line here is that it would not have happened if the people of the country did not want it. So, you have spoken. You definitely want casino gambling. Now learn something about it so it won't break you.

Testimonials for Previous Edition
Win At The Casino

I purchased your book, *Win At The Casino*, about six months ago. At that time I had already been gambling for a couple of months and I was losing more than I was winning. So what I was looking for, was a book that would cover all the basics, plus put me on the path to success. Fortunately for me your book did both.

I guess what I liked the most about your book was that it was easy to read, and easy to understand. But the most important thing was that you made it very clear as to what games to avoid, and how to cut your losses when things aren't going too good. The game I enjoy the most is blackjack, and what you said made a lot of sense. If a guy can just understand the basics, and you made that pretty easy, and then apply some of your money management techniques, he stands a pretty good chance of either making some money or cutting his losses. I know it's tough to win all the time, but your book has helped me in a big way, and so I just wanted to write to say THANK YOU VERY MUCH.

Paul Bruning
Colorado

I found a copy of your book, *Win At the Casino*, in my lunchroom a couple of weeks ago. One of my employees had brought it in to study on his breaks. So, being a semi-professional gambler, I picked it up and started reading. Not because I expected to find something new, because I've gambled in casinos since the early 80's, and I have already read nearly everything in print about the subject. Frankly, I just wanted to see if your book contained as much B.S. as most of them. Much to my surprise, it did not.

In fact, especially when I read your tips, I was reminded of a number of points that I had been overlooking for the past several years. In other words, I already knew those things, but had been failing to apply them. So, from that standpoint alone, I was very pleased. Sometimes I am amazed that I can know so much about something like Blackjack or Craps, and then forget to do the things that will make me a winner. All of us, I think, fall into traps created by bad habits, and your book helped me recognize some elementary errors I have been making. So this letter is just my way of saying thanks. I did read all the book, and think it's terrific for beginners, and even guys like me can learn something from reading it.

John Hosack
Colorado

Editor's Statement

If you like to gamble for fun but have no expectation of winning, there is good news for you. *Win at the Casino* allows you to leave the casino with a profit. If you want to really have fun and win at the casino, place this book into your personal collection.

To win, you have to act, think and play like a winner. Professional gambler and casino champion Dennis R. Harrison offers inside advice, betting tips and winning strategies to beat the casino.

When you gamble you need to have the right mental approach, the right attitude and the proper thinking process flowing through your mind. You not only play against the house rules, the casino odds and the other players — you play against yourself.

Whatever your game, winning is easy with *Win at the Casino*. You can now use the casino for your own profit — instead of letting it use you!

This is the most up-to-date and complete guide to betting and gambling. It offers a clear 3-point attack: win by playing the odds and knowing the rules; succeed by managing your money; and excel by using a solid mental approach to betting.

Of course, Lifetime Books does not advocate gambling with money you cannot afford to lose. Risking your next paycheck or life savings is not the way to go. If you have some spare cash to gamble with, do it wisely. Of course we cannot guarantee your winnings any more than Las Vegas handicappers can guarantee a winning prediction, but you are definitely on the right path by applying the strategies offered in this book.

Remember, play it smart, play the odds.

We wish you lots of luck!

--Brian Feinblum
Senior Editor
Lifetime Books

Chapter 1

Blackjack

I begin with Blackjack for a very simple reason: The odds can be more favorable for the player than in any other game. In fact, there are those who think that anyone who does not select Blackjack as his or her specialty is a masochist. The game is simple to play, the rules are clear and understandable. Properly played, the odds can actually be turned to the player's advantage.

I'll start with a basic description of the game. Some authors indicate that if you already know the basics, you should skip over this section and go on to the next, but I disagree. Even if you already know how the game is played, or *think* you know, read this section. It can't hurt and it might help. I will assume that you are entering a casino for the first time and want to try your luck at Blackjack.

Your first step is to find a table. Not just any table, but a table where the game is being played for stakes you can tolerate. It is quite embarrassing to rush up to a table, ask for $20 in chips, and then discover that the minimum bet at that table is $100.

You will usually find a small sign, to the dealer's right or left, which will indicate the minimum and maximum allowable wagers at that table. If the sign is obscured by ashtrays and empty drinks, don't hesitate to approach the dealer and inquire directly. Or, simply check the bets being made by the players. If all you see are green chips, it is probably a

$25 table (the minimum bet is $25). If all you see are red chips, it is undoubtedly a $5 table. If you see silver dollars or silver dollar tokens, it could be a $1, $2, or $3 table. Assuming that you are a novice, you'll want to start with low stakes; if your hotel/casino does not offer a low-minimum table, go somewhere else.

This, however, may pose a problem, particularly if you are gambling in Atlantic City, where you may have trouble finding even a $5 table. If, in fact, you want to start the learning process with bets of less than $5, you would be better off planning a vacation to Las Vegas, Reno, or even some Riverboats where $2 or $3 tables may still be found.

Figure 1 shows a typical table. Your first preference should be to sit at the seat labeled "Third base" (the reason for this will be explained later), but any seat will do. Regardless, I'll assume you've found a table to your liking. Now it's time to dig into your wallet or purse and bring out the greenbacks. And let me emphasize that you will, indeed, be playing for money. In reality, you will be playing with the chips your money has bought, but too many people forget that those red, green, and black chips represent authentic United States dollars; in most cases, hard-earned dollars.

On my first trip to Las Vegas, I was playing Blackjack within 35 minutes of my arrival. I played from eight o'clock in the evening until two o'clock the next afternoon, consuming great quantities of free drinks in the process. And I made a fatal mistake. During that playing session, I forgot that I was playing for money. I was not making $5-$25 bets, I was playing with nifty-looking red and green chips. I was not losing money, I was losing chips. Mentally, I had made a fundamental blunder. The chips didn't mean anything to me. They were simply playthings; toys. That is, they were simply playthings until I finally quit and discovered that those playthings added up to $475 in losses! I have never made that mistake again. It was an expensive lesson.

Do not forget that you are playing for real money. You are *not* playing a friendly game of Monopoly. The casinos claim it is much easier and faster for the dealer to work with chips instead of cash, and that is true. It is also true, however, that people tend to forget about money when they are playing with chips.

Also, why do you think the casinos serve free drinks to anyone who is gambling? You can answer that question for yourself.

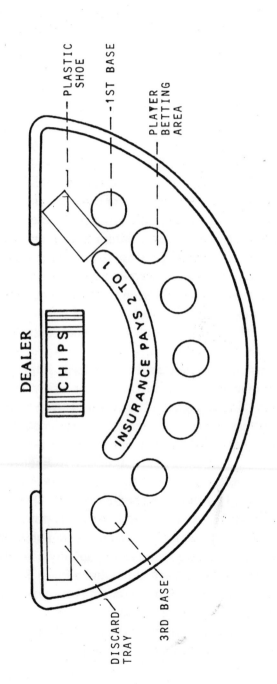

PLASTIC SHOE

1ST BASE

PLAYER BETTING AREA

INSURANCE PAYS 2 TO 1

DEALER

CHIPS

DISCARD TRAY

3RD BASE

FIGURE ONE

Another suggestion: Purchase only a few chips. If you are playing at a $2 table, don't start with more than $20. If at a $5 table, don't start with more than $30-$40. Do not buy $100 worth of chips simply because you have a hundred dollar bill. You are not going to impress anyone, and you will not intimidate the dealer by dropping a hundred dollar bill on the table. Go to the cashier, break your hundred dollar bill into five twenties and *then* buy chips at the Blackjack table.

There are several reasons why I make this suggestion. First, having too many chips in front of you can create a false sense of security; as long as you can look down and see chips on the table, you will have a tendency to keep playing, even though you may be losing badly. Second, and conversely, if you only start with a small amount, and those chips suddenly vanish, you will have an automatic alarm clock to help make you aware that you are, indeed, losing money. There will be times when you can sit at a table and do everything right, but still lose. The trick is to conserve your losses when you are losing. So, if that first $20 or $30 disappears, change tables! A new table can improve your morale and may help change your luck. In addition, your first time at the Blackjack tables will be an experiment of sorts. You're going to find out if you really understand the game, so don't make it an expensive training session.

To purchase chips, simply wait until the dealer is finished with the hand being played, place your $20 in front of or to the side of your playing spot, and say "Change, please" or "Chips, please". Most times you will not need say anything. The dealer will automatically collect your cash and trade you for chips. Do not place the money *on* your playing (betting) area. This may lead the dealer to believe that you want to make a $20 cash bet. Some dealers will ask whether you want to bet that $20, others will go ahead and begin the deal. Don't leave any room for misunderstanding. Also, if the dealer does not give you the chips you want, tell her (I'll assume your dealer is female). If, for example, the dealer gives you four $5 chips and you only want to play for $2 a hand, push two of the chips back at her and request $1 chips.

Another point: The dealer can give you chips for your money, but the same is not true in reverse. She cannot buy back your chips when you leave the table. Chips can only be exchanged for money at the cashier's cage.

Okay, now you have your chips; probably two $5 chips and ten $1 chips. To make your initial wager, place the minimum bet in your playing area (see Figure One). On some tables this area is rectangular, on others it is circular. Your chips should be stacked neatly, one on top of the other. When you see the dealer reminding people to stack their bets, it is not because she is a tidy person. It is because it is more difficult for a cheater to swindle the casino if the chips are stacked properly.

If you are making an odd wager, say $37, the chips should be stacked in the following manner: The largest-value chips on the bottom, the smallest-value on the top, and any others in the middle. If betting a green $25 chip, two red $5 chips, and two silver dollar tokens, the green would be on the bottom, the reds in the middle, the tokens on top. The casinos insist on this to help prevent cheating by the players. If this sounds a little strange, let me explain. Let's say you want to swindle the casino. You look at your first two cards, discover a total of twenty, and decide you have a very good chance of winning the hand. So, with lightning-fast fingers, you quickly add a few more chips to your bet while the dealer is concentrating on another player. Yes, I know that sounds silly. Who could possibly move that fast? No one could possibly get away with such a trick. Right? Wrong. Dealers and pit bosses tell me that people try to do it all the time. In our $37 example, with your chips stacked properly, you'd only be able to add a few dollars to the top of your bet, which would hardly be worth the effort. But, were the chips stacked so that the $25 chip was on top of the pile, you could easily add another $50 or $100, which to some people might be worth the risk of getting caught. And that's why you must stack your chips properly.

What happens next depends on how many decks are in use at your table. There are single-deck tables, double-deck tables, four-deck tables, and even six-deck tables. Who knows? One day we might even see eight- or ten-deck tables. The more decks, the more benefit to the casinos. Personally, I prefer single- or double-deck tables. Other gamblers will disagree with me, but I believe that anyone who plays at a four- or six-deck table is deranged. Though it is possible to win with four or six decks, it is much more difficult than it is playing with one or two decks. If your hotel casino does not offer single or double decks, go somewhere else.

If you are in doubt as to how many decks are being used, ask the dealer. If there is a "shoe" (see Figure 1) on the table, at least four decks are being used. A "shoe" is a small plastic box which holds all the cards. Instead of dealing from her hands, the dealer slides the cards out of the shoe.

Now for the cards. It's a new shuffle. The dealer carefully mixes the cards, flips a red plastic card at you, then holds the shuffled decks in front of your playing position. Yes, that's right. She wants you to cut the cards. That red card, sometimes yellow or green, is used to cut the deck. The dealer will extend all the decks so that you can insert the plastic card somewhere in the pile. The dealer then cuts the cards at that point.

After you've cut the cards, the dealer will discard the first one, two, or more cards into another small plastic tray to her right, called the "discard tray". This action is called "burning" a card. Later in this chapter I will explain its purpose.

The burning completed, the dealer starts dealing the cards from her left to her right, from first base to third base. In one- and two-deck games the player's cards are normally all dealt face down. In multiple-deck games the player's cards are often dealt face up. In either case, the dealer always has one card face up, one face down. The dealer's face-down card is called the "down" card or the "hole" card.

You watch your two cards slide toward you, pick them up, and make your first mistake. Thinking you were still at home playing with friends, you grab the cards with both hands. This is a no-no. A serious error! Should you make this mistake, do not be surprised if the dealer barks at you. For, you see, you can only touch the cards with *one* hand. Like most other casino rules, this one is to prevent cheating by the players. Should you be playing at a table where all the cards are dealt face up, you don't touch the cards at all.

So, you've got the cards in one hand. Time to calculate the value of your hand. Don't be rushed. Take your time. Not all of us are mathematically inclined, so don't get nervous if the dealer gives you an annoyed look. Each card has a point value. Tens, Jacks, Queens and Kings are worth ten points each. Aces can be either one or eleven. All other cards are face value; a Six is worth six points, a Two is worth two points, and so forth.

The object of the game is to obtain a total of 21, or as close to 21 as possible, without exceeding 21. If you exceed a total of 21, you "bust" (lose automatically). If you do not bust, and your total is higher than the dealer's total, you win even money. For example, a $5 bet would win $5. Should your total be the same as the dealer's total, you tie (or "push"), and neither win nor lose.

Assume your first hand is a Jack and an Ace. Rejoice! You have a natural Blackjack, a total of 21 on your first two cards, which is an automatic winner. Not only do you win, but the payoff is three to two. A $5 bet would win $7.50, a $10 bet would win $15, and so forth. A natural Blackjack is any two-card hand consisting of an Ace and any ten-value card. When you receive a natural, expose your cards immediately; turn them over and lay them down in front of your bet. If you're at a table where the cards are being dealt face up you needn't do anything but collect your winnings.

A natural Blackjack cannot lose, but it can be tied by a dealer natural. If the dealer's up card is an Ace, she must peek at her hold card to see if she has a natural. If she does, everyone loses except the players who also have naturals. Those players tie, or push.

Anyway, you won your first hand. Congratulations. You are smiling joyously, so the dealer grins at you and then turns to the player at first base. That player is the first to choose from several available options. Since you were dealt a natural you don't need to exercise any options, but you still need to understand your alternatives. Here they are:

1) You can *stand* (or *stick*, or *stand pat*). This means that you are satisfied with your first two cards and don't want any more. To stand in a game where the cards are dealt face down, you simply slide your cards under the chips in your betting area. However, you *must not* actually touch the chips with your hands; the casino might think that you're cheating. If the cards are all dealt face up, simply wave your hand over the cards with your palm parallel to the table.

You may also say, "I'm good", or "No more for me", or words to that effect. However, virtually all casinos prefer that you use hand signals, and some demand that you do so. For, you see, all of your intentions are clearly recorded by the overhead cameras. So make it easy for all concerned and use plain hand signals at all times.

2) You may request additional cards (or *hit*, or *draw*). This means that you are not happy with your first two cards and want to improve your total. If the cards were dealt face down, hold the cards in your hand and brush them lightly against the top of the table. The dealer will give you another card every time you make this motion. If the cards were all dealt face up, you can accomplish the same by brushing your index finger on the table as if your finger were a dog who is digging for a bone. If by taking additional cards you exceed a total of 21, you bust. In that case you must expose all your cards by laying them face up on the table. The dealer will then collect your cards and your losing wager. You can take as many additional cards as you want as long as you do not exceed 21. When you are through taking cards, you then stand as noted in #1 above.

3) You can *double down*. Explained later.

4) You can *split*. No, this doesn't mean you can grab your money and run for the exit, even though your initial two cards may inspire that reaction. I'll cover this one later, also.

5) You can *surrender*. Later.

6) You can buy *insurance*. Later.

As you watch the dealer move from player to player, you'll see your fellow gamblers exercising these options. When all the players have acted on their hands, it's the dealer's turn. Ah, the poor dealer. While the players have several options, the dealer has only two:

1) If the dealer's total is 16 or less, she *must* take additional cards until she totals from 17 to 21 or busts.

2) If the dealer's total is 17 or more, she *may not* take additional cards.

After acting on her hand, the dealer then settles all wagers, usually working from third base back to first base. Then the next round begins. You place your bet, receive your cards, decide which option to exercise, and win or lose. See, I told you this was simple.

What makes Blackjack so interesting to play is that the gamblers have many options, the dealer only two. For the person who enjoys making quick decisions, no other casino game is as challenging or rewarding.

But how do you know when to exercise the various options? Are there bad times to stand, good times to hit? And if you exercise your options properly, can you actually win? Yes, yes, and yes.

The following sections set forth the strategy you should use to win at Blackjack. You *must* study the charts, memorize and practice them if you are serious about winning. You cannot win by exercising your options with decisions based only on intuition or lucky feelings. You *must* know the basic strategies in this book. They may seem difficult at first, so take your time. You can learn them!

HARD HOLDINGS

I don't know how the term originated, but it is quite descriptive. Often a hard holding of 12-16 puts you between arock and a hard spot, creates a hard lump in your throat, or causes you to cast a very hard, disgusted look at the dealer.

A hard holding (also called *hard hand* or *stiff*) is a holding which can only be counted in one manner. A holding of Queen, Six can only be counted as 16. A holding of Eight, Seven can only be counted as 15. All hands are hard hands unless one or both of your cards is an Ace, since Aces can be one or eleven.

What do you do if you have a total of 15 and the dealer's up card is an Ace? What if the dealer is showing a Two or a Six? Sometimes the decisions are agonizing.

The chart which follows tells you what to do in every instance with Hard Holdings. Study it, memorize it, test yourself on it. Don't worry, you can learn it. I have tested this strategy in over a hundred thousand actual hands, plus used it in over a quarter million practice hands. It works.

HARD HOLDING STRATEGY
S=STAND   H=HIT   *=OPTIONAL

THE DEALER IS SHOWING: YOU HAVE	2	3	4	5	6	7	8	9	10	ACE
4-11	H	H	H	H	H	H	H	H	H	H
12	H	H	S	S	S	H	H	H	H	H
13	S	S	S	S	S	H	H	H	H	H
14	S	S	S	S	S	H	H	H	H	H
15	S	S	S	S	S	H	H	H	H	H
16	S	S	S	S	S	H	H	H	*	H
17-21	S	S	S	S	S	S	S	S	S	S

Figure 2

There, that's not so difficult, is it? If you have 12 and the dealer is showing a Seven, you hit. If you have 12 and the dealer's up card is a Six, you stand. I give you an option on 16 versus a dealer Ten because this decision is never right, never wrong. If you have a total of 11 or less, hit. Stand on any total of 17 or more.

But, you also ask, why do I hit when I'm holding 12 and the dealer is showing an Ace, stand when the dealer is showing a Six, hit when the dealer is showing a Two? Good questions, all. The answers lie in Figures 3 and 4 which follow.

DEALER IS SHOWING	% OF TIME DEALER WILL FINISH WITH 17 TO 21	% OF TIME DEALER WILL BUST
Ace	83%	17%
10	77%	23%
9	77%	23%
8	76%	24%
7	74%	26%
6	58%	42%
5	57%	43%
4	60%	40%
3	62%	38%
2	70%	30%

Figure 3

YOUR TOTAL IS	% OF TIME YOU CAN HIT WITHOUT BUSTING	% OF TIME A HIT WILL BUST YOU
11 or less	100.0%	00.0%
12	69.2%	30.8%
13	61.5%	38.5%
14	53.8%	46.2%
15	46.2%	53.8%
16	38.5%	61.5%
17	30.7%	69.3%
18	23.1%	76.9%
19	15.4%	84.6%
20	7.7%	92.3%

Figure 4

The percentages in Figures 3 and 4 will vary as the game progresses, but not much. Consequently, they are the percentages to use in determining whether to hit or stand. It is these percentages, combined with the rigid rules governing the dealer's options, which produce the basic strategy set forth in Figure 2. When the dealer has a high chance of busting, you do not want to hit. In those cases, you play for the dealer to bust. You want to shift the risk from your hand to the dealer's hand.

For example: Assume that your hand is 15. The dealer is showing a Nine. Figure 4 indicates that you have a 53.8% chance of busting, should you hit. However, Figure 3 indicates that the dealer will finish with 17-21 77% of the time. If you stand on your 15, you will probably lose. Therefore, in this case, you take the offensive in an attempt to improve your hand.

Now let's change the dealer's up card. Let's say she has a Five showing instead of a Nine. Figure 2 indicates that you should stand. The reasons are twofold: First, you have a 53.8% chance of busting if you hit. Second, the dealer has a 43% chance of busting. So why push your luck? Let the dealer risk busting *her* hand. You still may lose, but you've transferred the risk of busting to the dealer. Similar examples can be drawn for all the other hard holding totals, but I'll let you figure them out for yourself.

The basic strategy in Figure 2 does not change if your hand consists of more than two cards and you're playing against a shoe. If you have a three or four card total of 15, you should still hit against a dealer Nine. Assume you're playing against a shoe and you're dealt a Two and a Five. The dealer is showing a Queen. The basic strategy says to take a hit, so you do. You draw another Five, so now you've got a total of 12. The basic strategy says to hit a 12 against a dealer Queen; you do, and receive a Two, for a total of 14. Yes, I know you already have four cards, but that doesn't make any difference. Your lousy 14 will probably lose, so you must take another hit. You do, and receive an Ace. Now you have a 15 or 25, and since 25 is no good, you really have a hard 15. The sweat begins to trickle off your brow. The basic strategy says to hit a hard 15 when the dealer is showing any ten-value card. But you already have five cards, and you're convinced that if you take another hit you'll bust your hand. Your mind screams for you to stand pat. The other players are staring at you, waiting to see if you are stupid enough to draw a sixth card. It's decision time. And, since the basic strategy says to take a hit, you do so. Unfortunately, you receive a Ten and bust the hand, thereby losing your bet. Well, what can I say? You're not going to win every hand. The basic strategy is a guide which will help, but it will not miraculously cause you to win all the time. You might have caught a Six and won. That's why it's called "gambling". Nothing ventured, nothing gained. However, in single and double deck games I prefer to stand on any three-card 15 or 16.

Whenever you are dealt an initial holding of 12, 13, 14, 15, or 16, your odds of winning are very slim. Again, that's why those totals are called hard holdings or stiffs. They are bad for your morale and bad for your pocketbook. Consequently, the strategy in Figure 2 is designed to make the best out of terrible situations.

As I stated earlier in this chapter, it is possible to do everything right and still lose. But if you use the basic strategy you will lose less than the other players at your table who are relying solely on luck or whimsy. And I'm not discarding luck as being a valuable asset. What I'm saying is this: If you are using the basic strategy and you are still losing, you don't have any luck. Your karma is bad. Fate has decided to rob you of your money. You can't buck bad odds and bad luck. The basic strategy will help turn the odds in your favor and also protect you against the horrendous losses commonly associated with "bad luck". But if you sit down at a Blackjack table and continually receive 12's, 13's, 14's, 15's and 16's, you are playing the wrong game. Leave the table and visit the hotel's steam room. If you use the basic strategy and still lose, you'll know fate is being unkind. If you *do not* use the basic strategy, there is no way to determine whether your losses are the result of bad luck or poor, foolish card play. On too many occasions to count, I have observed players making numerous ridiculous plays at the Blackjack tables, and then heard those same gamblers complain about not having any luck. Play wisely, and you can create your own luck.

Yes, you will win some of the time when you have hard holdings. Yes, it is even possible to win a majority of those hands. However, the odds are against you, overall. If, in fact, you are winning a majority of those hands, you may wish to increase your bets. You could be on a "hot streak", or the dealer could be on a "cold streak".

In the next sections you'll see that there are ways for you to make up for all those terrible hard holding hands, options which will mean money in your pocket if utilized properly. On the hard holding hands, you are really striving to break even. On the other hands you swing the odds in your favor.

DOUBLING DOWN

Perk up, your odds of winning are now improving. Pray that each new hand brings a double down opportunity. If you double down in the correct situations you can recapture the money you lost on all those miserable 15's and 16's. Here's your chance to get even with the dealer for giving you all those bad hands.

The term "doubling down" derives from two actions. First, you double your bet; second, you receive one additional card, normally dealt face down. Hence, you double down.

The rules governing doubling down vary from area to area. Most casinos allow you to double down on any two-card holding, others only on a holding of 10 or 11. It is to your advantage to play at casinos which allow you to double down on *any* two-card holding.

To double down, you must expose your cards to the dealer by placing them face up in front of your betting area. Then you match your original bet with a like amount placed *adjacent* to your original bet. If your original wager was $5, you must extend another $5. If all the cards were dealt face up, simply match your original wager. The dealer will then give you one card. You do not have the option of taking more cards. You receive one card, and one card only. Sound risky? It *is* if you do it at the wrong times; it *is not* if you do it at the right time. The chart depicted in Figure 5 will tell you when the time is right.

DOUBLING DOWN
D=DOUBLE DOWN   H=HIT

THE DEALER IS SHOWING:	2	3	4	5	6	7	8	9	10	ACE
YOU HAVE										
11	D	D	D	D	D	D	D	D	D	D
10	D	D	D	D	D	D	D	D	H	H
9	D	D	D	D	D	H	H	H	H	H

Figure 5

You should double down on 11 against every dealer up card, on 10 against every dealer up card except a Ten or an Ace, on 9 only when the dealer is showing a Six or less. If you compare Figure 5 with Figure 3, you'll see how the doubling down strategy was developed. In essence, you want to double down whenever the dealer has a high probability of busting. Doubling on 11 against a dealer Seven, Eight, Nine, Ten, or Ace is an offensive attempt. Remember that in a deck of 52 cards there are sixteen ten-value cards (four Tens, four Jacks, four Queens, and four Kings), so your chance of receiving a ten-value card on your double down is good. Also, you only want to double down on holdings which cannot be busted by the addition of one card; you would *not* double down on 12, 13, 14, or more.

I know one gambler who doubles down each time he has less than 12 and the dealer is showing a Five or a Six. Yes, I've seen him double down on a holding of 5. And, believe it or not, he wins more than he loses. However, when I tried the same strategy I was massacred. In any case, you don't want to be too greedy. Don't forget: When you double down you double your winnings, but you can also double your losses. Use doubling down wisely and you'll give yourself an edge over the casino.

SOFT HOLDINGS

A "soft" holding is any holding which can be counted in *more than one* manner. This can only happen when you have an Ace in your hand. Remember, an Ace can be counted as *either* one or eleven. If you have a holding of Ace, Five you have either 6 or 16. Since a holding of 16 is tantamount to certain death, you should count the Ace as one, for a total of 6.

If you have a holding of Ace, Nine, you will want to count the Ace as eleven, for a total of 20. You may also count it as one, for a total of 10, but why reduce a potential winning hand to an unknown?

Ace, Four could be 5 or 15. Ace, Seven could be 8 or 18. Obviously, having a soft holding gives you more flexibility. It is virtually impossible to bust a soft holding. But, ordinarily, a soft holding does not stay soft very long.

Assume you're dealt Ace, Five. You treat the Ace as a value of one, so your total is 6. You take a hit (you can't possible bust) and catch a

King. Your hand is no longer soft. Now you have a hard holding of 16 (1+5+10).

Another example: You are dealt Ace, Three. You have either 4 or 14. You take a hit and get a Two. Now you have Ace, Three, Two, which is worth either 6 or 16. You take another hit, an Eight. Ace, Three, Two, Eight totals 14. It must total 14. You have no other choice. If you treat you Ace as eleven, you total would be $11 + 3 + 2 + 8 = 24$!

Soft holdings can make for very interesting hands. I am sure that this has happened to all seasoned Blackjack players, but I will relate this experience as an example. I was at a crowded casino on New Year's Eve, and all the two-deck tables were busy. I was possessed by gambling fever, so, in a fit of stupidity, I decided to play at a six-deck table. On one hand, my initial two cards were Ace, Two. The dealer was showing a Ten. I took a hit. I received another Ace, giving me either 4(1+1+2) or 14(1+11+2). My second hit was another Ace, as was my third. My hand was then Ace, Ace, Ace, Ace, Two for either 6(1+1+1+1+2) or 16(1+1+1+11+2). I then took another hit and received yet another Ace. Remember, I was at a six-deck table, so there were twenty-four Aces in the shoe. Anyway, my six-card total was still only 7 or 17. I could have stopped at that point, but since the dealer was showing a Ten, and since I could not possible bust my hand with another hit, I brushed my cards on the felt and received a Five, which gave me a total of 12 (1+1+1+1+1+2+5). At that point, by soft holding finally became a hard holding. The interesting point is that my hand stayed soft for six cards, which does not happen very often.

In case you're interested in whether I won or lost that hand, I suppose I should finish the story. I had to take two more hits to complete my hand. One was a Deuce, the other was a Five. My final hand was Ace, Ace, Ace, Ace, Ace, Two, Five, Two, Five for a total of 19. The dealer had 18. Hurrah for our side!

Figure 6 shows you what to do with various soft holdings against all dealer up cards. With soft holdings you really have three options: stand, hit, or double down.

When you read Figure 6 you'll see many doubling down opportunities. The reasons for doubling down a soft holding are threefold: First, you cannot possible bust your hand. Second, in each of the situations depicted in Figure 6 there is an excellent probability of the dealer busting. Finally, there is a chance that you will receive a card which will improve your hand. So you have just enough of an edge to make it worthwhile to double your bet.

You always stand on Ace, Eight and Ace, Nine, because those hands are worth 19 and 20, respectively. You could double down on either of those hands against a dealer Five or Six, but again I caution you against becoming greedy. Unless, that is, you're on a hot streak, which is definitely the time to be as greedy as Scrooge.

Explore this chart, study it, memorize it and compare it with Figure 3. You'll see that some of the situations call for defensive action, others for offensive action by the player. As with the chart for doubling down, astute use of soft holdings will increase your winnings.

SOFT HOLDINGS
S=STAND   H=HIT   D=DOUBLE DOWN

THE DEALER IS SHOWING: 2 3 4 5 6 7 8 9 10 ACE

YOU HAVE

YOU HAVE	2	3	4	5	6	7	8	9	10	ACE
Ace,9	S	S	S	S	S	S	S	S	S	
Ace,8	S	S	S	S	S	S	S	S	S	
Ace,7	S	D	D	D	D	S	S	H	H	S
Ace,6	H	D	D	D	D	S	H	H	H	H
Ace,5	H	H	D	D	D	H	H	H	H	H
Ace,4	H	H	D	D	D	H	H	H	H	H
Ace,3	H	H	D	D	D	H	H	H	H	H
Ace,2	H	H	D	D	D	H	H	H	H	H

Figure 6

SPLITTING

When you split your initial two cards you actually turn one hand into two, with each treated as a separate hand which must be played. This can only happen when your first two cards are a pair. If your first two cards are Two, Two, you can split them. You can split Three, Three or Four, Four, or any pair including any two ten-value cards (Ten, Jack, or Queen, King).

Since you will now be playing two separate hands after splitting your cards, you must double your bet. The procedure is the same as that for doubling down; expose your cards to the dealer and match your bet with a like amount. If the cards were dealt face up, simply match your bet. But unlike doubling down, take care to create a space between your cards when you expose them. If you are splitting a pair and you lay them down so that one card is on top of the other, the dealer may think you want to double down. In any case, make sure the dealer understands that you want to split.

The dealer will issue a hit to the first card of your pair (the first of your two separate hands) and wait to see if you want additional cards on that hand. The hand is played like any other, using the strategies that were discussed. You can hit or stand, and the casinos which offer the best rules will also allow you to double down or resplit. Once the first hand is completed, the dealer moves to your second hand.

There are rule variations for splitting, but one rule is the same at all casinos. If you split a pair of Aces, you will receive only *one* card, usually dealt face down, on each of your Aces. You have no options. You live or die with the single card that you are dealt on each Ace. In addition, should one or both of your Aces be dealt a ten-value card, you do not have a natural Blackjack. You simply have a total of 21 and are paid even money if you win.

Remember, the only time you can have a natural Blackjack is on your initial two cards.

Here is the basic strategy for splitting:

SPLITTING PAIRS
S=STAND $=SPLIT   H=HIT   D=DOUBLE DOWN

THE DEALER IS SHOWING	2	3	4	5	6	7	8	9	10	ACE
YOU HAVE										
2,2	H	$	$	$	$	$	H	H	H	H
3,3	H	$	$	$	$	$	H	H	H	H
4,4	H	H	H	H	H	H	H	H	H	H
5,5	D	D	D	D	D	D	D	D	H	H
6,6	$	$	$	$	$	H	H	H	H	H
7,7	$	$	$	$	$	$	H	H	H	H
8,8	$	$	$	$	$	$	$	$	$	$
9,9	$	$	$	$	$	S	S	$	S	S
10,10	S	S	S	S	S	S	S	S	S	S
ACE,ACE	$	$	$	$	$	$	$	$	$	$

Figure 7

You should *always* split Ace, Ace and Eight, Eight. You should *never* split Ten, Ten or Five, Five. When holding Five, Five, you should use the rules for doubling down on Ten (see Figure 5). It is not a good idea to split Fours, but, if you feel lucky or are experiencing a hot streak, you can split them against a dealer Five or Six.

You will note that at times you are taking the offensive, at other times the defensive. Holding Seven, Seven is no great joy. By splitting Sevens you may draw cards which will improve your chance of winning (nearly anything is better than 14). Splitting Nines is an offensive attempt when the dealer is showing a card worth Six or less. Yet we do not split Nines against a dealer Seven for the simple reason that if the dealer has 17, you will beat her with your 18. Against a dealer Eight you should stand on Nine, Nine, hoping for a tie. Against a dealer Ten or Ace assume that your 18 will lose, so you split and try to save the bet by making a least one of the hands a winner. If one of the Nines draws a Two and a Ten you are in good shape even if you bust the other hand (you win one, lose one, and break even).

Splitting opportunities do not present themselves very often, but you should know how to handle them when they occur.

INSURANCE

This is one of the least understood of all the player options. Yet it can be quite beneficial once you know what buying insurance really means.

The only time you can buy insurance is when the dealer's up card is an Ace. In that case the dealer will ask all the players whether they want to buy insurance. If you want to buy insurance, place an amount equal to half your original wager into the area marked insurance (see Figure 1). The dealer then peeks at her hold card to see if she has a ten-value card for a natural Blackjack. If she does have a Blackjack, you lose your original wager(unless you also have a natural Blackjack), but you win two to one on your insurance bet. Had your original bet been $10, the insurance wager would have cost you $5. So you would lose your original wager of $10, but win $10 on your insurance bet, thereby breaking even. If the dealer does not have a Blackjack, you lose your insurance bet and the game continues in the normal manner, with each player then acting on their hands.

But you are *not* really buying insurance. In essence, you are simply making another bet. You are *betting* on whether or not the dealer has a natural Blackjack. And unless you are a card counter (explained later) this is a bad bet to make! Unless you are a card counter, there is only one possible instance when you *might* want to buy insurance . . . if you have a holding of 20. In that case, even if you lose the insurance bet you stand a good chance of winning your original wager. If you had bet $5 you would lose $2.50 on the insurance bet but would win $5 on the original wager, for a net gain of $2.50.

No matter what the dealers try to tell you, no matter what other players try to tell you, buying insurance is not a good bet unless you are a card counter. Some people will tell you that if you have a natural Blackjack as your holding you should always buy insurance. Or, in most casinos you can simply say "Even money!". What this means is that instead of receiving a payoff of 3:2 for your natural Blackjack, you receive a payoff of 1:1. You give up a third of your potential profit. However, should the dealer also have a natural Blackjack, you then have profit instead of a tie. My opinion is this: Go for the money! Why do you think the casinos allow players to call out "Even money!"? Because it is to their advantage to do so. And, yes, you guessed it, anything which benefits the casino is bad for us players. My advice is to never take even money on a natural Blackjack unless you are a card counter. In fact, I don't recommend buying insurance at any time, unless you are a card counter.

SURRENDER

Yes, this player option is exactly what the word implies. You surrender your hand to the dealer. You give up. You wave a white flag over your head. And the result is that the dealer takes only *half* your wager. If you are a card counter this option can be very beneficial. If you are not a card counter this option may not be as great as it sounds.

To surrender your cards, simply turn them over and expose them to the dealer. If the cards were all dealt face up, simply say "Surrender" or "I surrender". In either case, *do not* touch your bet. The dealer will take half of your wager. The casino does not want you fooling around with your chips because, as I've already stated several times, they are always on guard for cheaters.

You may only exercise this option *before* acting on your hand. You cannot take a hit, bust, and then surrender. You must surrender your original two cards.

If you are not a card counter, there are only a few situations in which you *might* want to surrender. If your hand is 15 or 16 and the dealer is showing a ten-value card; or if your hand is a 14 made up of Seven, Seven and the dealer is showing a ten-value card. Otherwise, take your chances and try to beat the dealer.

Not all casinos offer this option, so always ask the dealer whether it is available.

CARD COUNTING

Card counting means counting certain cards in order to ascertain whether the deck is in favor of the players or the dealer. Yes, a deck of cards can fluctuate quite a bit in favor of one or the other. It has been conclusively proven by numerous mathematical studies that the deck is favorable to the players when the ratio of high cards remaining in the deck is greater than the ratio of low cards. When the deck contains a high ratio of low cards, Twos through Sixes, the dealer gets very tough. When the deck contains a high ratio of high cards, ten-values and Aces, it's the player's turn to multiply his or her winnings.

If you are not a card counter, you may have even confused a favorable deck with "luck". Assume that you play at a six-deck table and that, by the time you begin to play, the majority of the low cards have already been played. You then win five hands in a row and decide that your luck is good. But, in fact, you won because the deck was favorable for the players. Of course, the reverse could also happen. You could sit down at a time when the deck is favorable for the dealer, lose five hands in a row, and decide that you have bad luck.

Card counting is not difficult. It *can* be very difficult if you use a complicated counting system, but exotic counting systems are best left to the experts. What you need is a system which is easy to use and easy to remember . . . a simple system which will help you win more and avoid losses. I will cover what I feel are the two easiest ways to count cards, and also a third, slightly more difficult option.

Counting Ten-Values

If you watch closely, whether the cards are dealt face up or face down, you will see every card that is played when players bust or when the dealer makes the settlements. All you must do is count the number of ten-value cards that you see. Will it help? Immensely! Is it worth the effort? Absolutely!

There are 52 cards in each deck, sixteen of which are ten-values. This means that approximately one of every three cards is a ten-value. If the deck is "even" (the ten-values are spread equally through the deck), one ten-value should be played for about every three cards. When only a few ten-values are dealt on a hand, the next round will be "rich" in ten-values. When a lot of ten-values are dealt on a hand, the next round should be "poor" in ten-values. If the deck is rich, the benefit is to the players. If the deck is poor, the benefit is to the dealer.

Common sense would tell us that, if the deck is rich in ten-values, the dealer has the same opportunity of being dealt a good hand as the players, and common sense would be correct. Just because the deck is rich in ten-values, you will not necessarily be dealt a pair of ten-values on the next hand. It might be the dealer who catches that pair of ten-values. So how does counting ten-values, knowing whether the deck is rich or poor, improve our chances for earning a profit?

Example: The dealer is showing a ten-value. You have 11. The basic strategy says you should double down. However, from counting the ten-values, you know that the deck is very poor in ten-values. Should you still double down? Absolutely not!

Example: The dealer is showing a ten-value. You have a hard holding of 15. The basic strategy says to hit. But you know that the deck is very rich in ten-values. Should you still take a hit? No! You are almost certain to bust. Cross your fingers and hope the dealer doesn't have another ten-value for her hole card.

Example: The dealer shows an Ace, and asks if you want to buy insurance. You know that the deck was very rich in ten-values at the start of that round. Should you buy insurance? Of course.

Example: The dealer is showing a ten-value, a Nine, an Eight, or a Seven. Your have a miserable 15. You know that the deck is rich in ten-values. Should you hit? Stand? No, you should do neither. This is a perfect example of when you should surrender, if you have that option.

Example: The dealer is showing a Five. You have a holding of 8. You know that the deck is rich in ten-values. Should you hit? No! Instead, you could double down. The dealer's chance of busting is even greater than normal, so take your best shot.

By counting ten-values, you can modify the basic strategies to greatly increase your advantage over the dealer, and dramatically increase your odds of winning.

Here's an easy way to count ten-values. I have found that, on the average, 3.2 cards are used by each player during each round. Some will play with their initial two cards, others will take multiple hits, but the average is usually 3.2 per player. One out of every 3.25 cards in the deck is a ten-value. This means that you should see, or count, one ten-value for each player, including the dealer, at your table on each round. And, by the way, I don't consider the deck to be rich or poor unless the ten-value count is at least three more or three less than what it should be.

Example: Six players plus the dealer. On the first hand of a new shuffle you count twelve ten-values. Is the deck rich or poor for the next round? Figure it out. Six players + the dealer = seven people. Seven ten-values should have been played; one for each player and one for the dealer. Since twelve were actually played, the remaining deck is very poor in ten-values.

Example: You are playing at a table with four other gamblers. For some undetermined reason, you are playing against a shoe of six decks. On the first round of cards you count three ten-values, on the second round you count only two ten-values, and on the third round you count six ten-values. Is the deck rich or poor in ten-values for the next round? Here's how to figure it out. You + four other gamblers + the dealer = a total of six people. So, approximately six ten-values should be played on each round. Three rounds of play should have seen eighteen ten-values. But how many did you count? Three + two + six = eleven. Consequently, the deck at that point is very rich in ten-values. Another benefit to knowing if the deck is rich or poor is that you can bet accordingly. If the deck is rich, to your advantage, you should increase your bet slightly. If the deck is poor, make a minimum wager.

Note: If there is too much fluctuation in your bets, particularly if you are winning, the fact that you are a card counter will be obvious to the casino personnel. To destroy your count, the casino will then either have the dealer reshuffle after every hand, or even ask you to leave. However, unless you are changing your bets from, say, $10 to $500, you need not worry about being tossed out of any casinos.

A good rule of thumb is that your maximum wager should not be more than three to four times your normal minimum bet. Some people recommend that your maximum bet should not exceed five times your normal wager, but I've found that if you suddenly increase your bet from, say, $10 to $50, you become a closely-watched gambler. Even worse, if you bet $10 on one hand, $50 on the next hand, then drop back down to $10 again, it's obvious you're either a counter or sick of mind. If you win that $50 bet, you're a counter. If you lose it, you're sick of mind. So take my advice. If you normally bet $5 on each hand, your largest bet should be $20. If you normally bet $10 on each hand, your largest bet should be $40. Of course there are exceptions to this rule, such as when you are using a progressive betting system. But using a progressive betting system will not brand you as a counter.

If you are counting ten-values and you begin to gain confidence, here's a suggestion. I'll assume you are varying your bets from $5 to $20. Instead of wagering $5 when the deck is even (neither rich nor poor), bet $10. Then, when the deck is poor you can drop down to a $5 wager, when rich go up to $20. The reasons are twofold. First, varying your bets by one unit up or down will not cause anyone to think you are a counter. Even if they do, bets of this spread will not worry the pit crew or set off any alarms. Second, knowing the richness or poorness of the deck gives you enough additional knowledge to increase to $10, even if the deck is just even. Once you're comfortable with counting ten-values, you're a smarter player, so you can afford to wager a little more.

Counting ten-values is an easy way to help turn the odds in your favor, but it is not an exact science. However, knowing whether the deck is rich or poor gives you that extra bit of information which will add winnings to your gambling stake, or . . . and this is just as important . . . help protect you from unnecessary losses.

Just remember this: The deck can only be "rich", "poor", or "even". If it's even, you would continue to use the basic strategy outlined earlier in this chapter. If it is rich or poor, use your common sense. There are only a few minor adjustments that need to be made if the deck is rich or poor, and these have already been covered in the examples.

Counting Aces

This will not help as much as counting ten-values, but when the deck is rich in Aces you have an increased opportunity of being dealt a natural Blackjack. Also, when the deck is rich in Aces you have more opportunity of being dealt a soft holding, which gives you much more flexibility. And when the deck is rich in Aces, doubling down on a holding of 9 or 10 makes for an even greater chance for success.

In addition, if you can manage to count both Aces *and* ten-values, you could be one of the best informed players in the casino. Try it sometime; it's not that difficult. Or play with a friend. You can count the ten-values, your friend can count the Aces.

One in every thirteen cards should be an Ace. So how many players are in the game? How many cards have been dealt? How many were Aces? Is the deck rich or poor in Aces? Use your head and figure it out for yourself.

Every time the deck is rich in ten-values *and* Aces, people are invariably dealt natural Blackjacks. It never fails. So, whenever I note that the deck is rich in Aces and ten-values, I make my largest bet. You would be amazed at how many times I've been dealt a natural Blackjack with a maximum bet on the table. And don't forget, a natural Blackjack is paid off at three to two instead of even money.

Aces are powerful cards, even though few in number. Listen closely the next time you play Blackjack. Sometime during your gambling session, one of your fellow gamblers will receive a natural Blackjack, moan, and then say something like this: "Damnit, I never have a big bet on the table when I catch a Blackjack. Seems like I always get them when I bet small."

Well, no kidding.

But *you*, the intelligent man or woman who is watching out for those precious Aces, will be prepared for those natural Blackjacks.

Positives and Negatives

For those of you who are willing to devote some time to serious card counting, here's your system. If you can master it, you'll be one of the toughest, hardest-to-beat Blackjack players in any casino. But let me warn you: It takes a *lot* of practice.

This system can be worked with infinite variations, so I'll explain the way I use it. And, by the way, I only use this system when I'm playing against a shoe. If I'm playing against one or two decks, I simply count ten-values and Aces. Not that counting ten-values and Aces is better, it's just less mentally demanding and fatiguing.

Count every ten-value card as worth minus one or negative one (-1). Count all Aces as worth negative two (-2). Assign all Threes, Fours, Fives and Sixes a value of positive one (+1). Do not bother to count Twos, Sevens, Eights or Nines. The object is to keep a running total as all the cards are played. If the running total is negative, the deck is in favor of the dealer. If the running total is positive, the deck is in favor of the players.

Think about it for a moment, and it will start to make sense. If the count is a positive number, a lot of low-value cards have been played, which then means the rest of the deck has a lot of high-value cards remaining in it. And you, as a player, want to be aware of situations when the deck is made up of a high ratio of high-value cards.

Try a few examples. The following cards are played: Ace, Three, Two, King. What's the count? The Ace is worth minus two(-2). The Three is worth positive one (+1). The Two has no value assigned to it, so don't count it. The King is worth minus one (-1). So what you have is, (-2) + (+1) + (-1). Added together, the count becomes a total of minus two (-2), which tells us that of the cards played thus far, more high-value cards have been played than low-value cards.

Another example. These cards are played: Jack, Four, Five, Seven, Eight, Three, King. What's the running count? This time add the totals just as you would in a real game. The Jack is a minus one (-1). The Four is a positive one (+1), so now the total is zero (0). The Five is a positive one (+1), so your total becomes positive one (+1). The Seven and the Eight do not count. The Three is a positive one (+1), so your total adds to positive two (+2). The King is a negative one (-1), which brings the running total back down to positive one (+1). In this example, your running total of positive one (+1) tells you that of all the cards played thus far, more low-value cards have been played than high-value cards.

Again, a positive running total tells you that the deck is composed of a favorable ratio of high-value cards. Positive means good, negative means bad for the players. The more often you have a positive running total, the more often you will win.

Now here's how to adjust your play based on this running total. I've found that the total must reach at least a count of four, whether positive or negative, before I make any changes in my bets or in the basic strategy. When that happens, here's what to do:

1) With a running count of plus four (+4), double your wager. If you've been betting $5, bet $10.
2) With a running count of plus six (+6) or more, triple your bet. If you've been wagering $5, wager $15.
3) With a running count of plus six (+6) or more:
   a) Double your bet after every winning hand. If you had bet $30, make your next bet $60. This will not indicate that you are counting cards, for the simple reason that gamblers often double up after a win.
   b) Always buy insurance if offered.

    c) Double down on all totals of 8 against all dealer Fours, Fives, and Sixes.

    d) Do not hit any hard holdings of 15 or 16.

    e) Surrender any hard holdings of 14, 15 or 16 against a dealer ten-value.

4) With a running count of minus four (-4):

    a) Do not double down on a holding of 11 unless the dealer is showing less than a ten-value.

    b) Do not double down on a holding of 10 unless the dealer is showing a Four, Five, Six or Seven.

    c) Do not split Aces unless the dealer is showing a Five or a Six.

    d) Never surrender any hand, regardless of how bad it seems.

The list could go on and on, but common sense should prevail. All these rules mean additional winnings or reduced losses, so try to remember them when you are using the Negative-Positive counting system. It is the most troublesome system to learn, but it is also the most accurate.

I should now explain two statements which I made earlier in this chapter. First, I indicated that, if at all possible, you should sit at third base. The reason for choosing that position is that by sitting at third base you are able to see, and therefore count, more cards before you need to exercise any options on your hand. This is beneficial even if you're not a card counter, but it is especially beneficial if you are utilizing a card-counting system. The more cards you can count, and the more accurate your count, the more you turn the odds in your favor.

Example: At the start of a round of play, you note that the deck is "rich" in high-value cards. Consequently, you know that the remaining portion of the deck should be favorable for the players. You are dealt a Seven and a Four. The dealer is showing a Queen. Since the remaining deck is composed of a high ratio of high-value cards, you anticipate doubling down. But you are seated at third base, and five or six players acting before you all take hits. They all receive ten-values. Would you still double down? Perhaps not. By the time it is your turn to exercise your options, the deck may no longer be "rich" in high-value cards.

Your second choice of places to sit should be at first base. The reason? At first base, you are able to exercise your options before all the other players. In the example stated above, had you been seated at first base, you would definitely have doubled down. Had you been at first base, the other players would not have depleted the high ratio of high-value cards remaining in the deck.

Now that I've told you why you should sit at first or third base, let me try to confuse you. Most card counters that I've met prefer first or third base. Most pit bosses know that most card counters prefer third or first base. Consequently, people who sit at third or first base tend to be watched more closely by the pit bosses, especially if the players in those two positions are winning consistently or varying their bets. So, while third and first base seats are preferable, don't feel cheated if you can't find one. In fact, there is nothing wrong with sitting in one of the middle seating positions. From the middle of the table it is actually easier to count cards, for the simple reason that you are midway between third and first bases and can therefore see all the cards with less difficulty. And now that you may be confused as to where you should sit, let me make one last statement: If you are a card counter, you should try to sit at third or first base. If you are a beginning card counter, if you are not adept at camouflaging your counting, or if you are not an expert, do not sit at third or first base.

I also mentioned earlier that dealers will "burn" one or more cards from the top of the deck or decks before beginning each new deal. Now that we're talking about card counting, I can tell you that the reason the top card (or cards) is "burned" is to make life more troublesome for card counters. When counting cards, it is imperative to see as many cards as possible. If the dealer burns the top four cards, and all four cards are ten-values, your count will never be entirely accurate. The more cards the casino burns, the more difficult it is to count cards.

I once played at a casino where the dealer burned the top eight cards from a four-deck shoe. I thought she had made a mistake, so I asked her if burning eight cards was a new policy at that casino. Her answer was, "Sometimes." Needless to say, I left that casino after a few hands. But before I exited, I noted that a lady sitting at third base was obviously a card counter. Unfortunately, she was making plays that few people would attempt, such as doubling down on a total of 7, and winning. So it became apparent that the dealer had burned eight cards in an attempt to discourage the counter.

While I'm thinking of it, here's another point I'd like to make. To my way of thinking, the players are all in a war against the dealer. No, that doesn't mean we should hate all dealers. To the extent that we players are all trying to win, it makes sense that we should help one another as much as possible. Therefore, if the cards are dealt face down, don't be afraid to let the players on either side of you see your cards. I am a card counter. So when the people around me try to conceal their cards so I can't see them, I sometimes become perturbed. The more cards I can see, the better my count, and the greater my chance of winning. Conversely, I always let the people around me see my cards, in the hope that a small amount of additional knowledge may help them. If I have a holding of 11 and everybody around me has two ten-value cards in their hand, I will certainly think twice before doubling down. Don't hide your cards from the other players!

Should you attempt to play the game of Blackjack without A) learning a good basic playing system, and/or B) without learning a counting system, the casinos will hold the edge on you of approximately 4-5%. Should you, however, learn a good basic playing system, like the one outlined earlier in this chapter, you can reduce the casino's advantage so it falls into the 0-1% range. And here's the best news of all: Should you learn both the basic playing system and a counting system, you can actually turn the edge to your favor. Not a lot, but at least in the 1-4% range. So, the question is this: Would you rather give up a 4% edge to the casino, or have that same 4% on your side? All it takes is a little effort.

MONEY MANAGEMENT

By this point, you should know the basic strategies and have an idea on how to count cards. Now let me make a statement: None of that means *anything*, unless you manage your money properly. You can play like a genius and still suffer horrendous losses if you don't protect your money by using the utmost care and diligence.

My suggestion is this: Don't bother sitting down to play unless you have at least fifty units. A unit could be $2 or $5 or $100, but, whatever it is, you should have fifty. If your unit is $2, fifty units would be $100. If your unit is $5 you should have $250. You must have at least fifty units to protect yourself against extended losing streaks, which *do* occur no matter how well you play.

Next, you *must* change tables if you lose four units. There are times when the composition of the deck is such that it favors the dealer for long stretches. This can be true whether you are playing with one deck, two decks, or multiple decks. Again, what some of you may think is "bad" luck can actually be caused by the composition of the cards. If the majority of the high-value cards are situated in the last half of the deck or decks, which is quite possible, then the first half of the deck or decks will greatly favor the dealer.

If you're playing with six decks, there are 312 total cards in the shoe, minus a few burn cards. Approximately half the decks, about 156 cards, will be played before the dealer reshuffles. If you are playing with four other gamblers, you could complete from eight to thirteen rounds of play before the deck is reshuffled. Therefore, if the composition of the decks is unfavorable, you could lose from eight to thirteen or more units, even if you play each hand perfectly. And it is also possible for the decks to contain the same composition for several hours at a time; that is, the decks could remain unfavorable for the players for long stretches of time. Why play against a dealer who is beating your brains out? I don't care if you need to change tables every five minutes . . . keep changing until you stop losing, keep changing until you find a table where the composition of the decks is more favorable.

Also, if you win as many as six units at any table, *do not* lose them all back! As soon as you start winning, put your original chips in your pocket and play with your winnings. Once you've won six units, don't you dare lose back more than three. Do not, at any time, allow the casino to win back more than half of your profits.

Lastly, if you're up as many as fifteen units, change your unit. If your unit was $5, for example, change it to $10. When you are winning, you must push for all you can. The player most feared by the casinos is the player who gradually increases his or her bets for maximum profits. If you increase your unit and start losing, go back to your original unit. If you win another fifteen units, increase your unit again. But one word of caution: If you are a $2 bettor and increasing your unit to $5 or $10 makes you nervous, stay with a lower unit. I know people who play faultlessly with $5 bets, but lose control if they increase to $15 or $25 bets.

RULE VARIATIONS

Not all casinos use the same rules governing the player and dealer options. What follows is a list of the differences which you may find. Remember to ask about the rules *before* you start playing.

1) *Doubling down*: In most casinos the player can double down on any initial two-card holding. However, there are also casinos which will allow you to double only on holdings of ten or eleven, which limits double down opportunities and is subsequently a disadvantage for the player.

2) *Splitting*: Some casinos allow pairs to be split and resplit; others allow splitting but no resplitting.

3) *Surrender*: This is an optional rule in Nevada and most other States, so ask everywhere you play.

4) *Doubling down after splitting*: Assume that you split a pair of Sixes and then receive a Five on the first Six. At most casinos, you may then double down on your 11. This is very beneficial to the player, so seek out casinos which offer this option.

5) *Dealer options*: In some casinos the dealer *must* stand on any 17. In others the dealer *may* stand on a soft 17 (Ace,Six). In still others, the dealer *must* hit a soft 17. It is to your advantage to play *only* where the dealer *must* stand on all 17's, whether soft or hard.

6) *Dealer Blackjacks*: At some casinos, if the dealer is showing a ten-value or Ace they must look at their hole card to determine whether they have a natural Blackjack. If they do, the game stops at that point. At others, the dealers are not allowed to peek at their hole card. Consequently, should you double down or split, only to find out later the dealer does have a natural Blackjack, you lose only your original wager.

7) *Double exposure*: In some casinos both the dealer's cards are dealt face up. This, of course, gives the player a tremendous advantage as it eliminates any speculation about the dealer's hole card. If the dealer is showing a total of 20, for example, you would hit your total of 19. But what the casinos give you with the right hand, they take back with the left. Here's what I mean. Though you have the advantage of seeing the dealer's hole card, in this game you are only paid even money if you receive a natural Blackjack. Also, most

casinos count all ties or "pushes" in this game as losses for the player. Only a fool would play against such heavy odds. If you haven't tried double-exposure Blackjack yet, you might want to try it at a one-dollar or two-dollar table, using your "fun" money. And make sure you know *all* the rules before you start making bets.

That's all for this chapter, but don't forget to read and study the practical advice in the last chapter of this book, which covers all the casino games. And even if you're not interested in Craps, Roulette, Baccarat, Caribbean Stud, etc., read the other chapters anyway. Who knows? You may want to play one of those games some day.

Chapter 2

Craps

This game intimidates far too many people. You see enthusiastic gamblers clustered around a large table with chips of all colors being thrown, shifted, placed and removed with alarming speed. The money changes hands so fast it is puzzling for the novice, and there are so many betting options that most people don't have the foggiest notion what is happening. Pass, Don't Pass, Come, Don't Come, Hard Eight, Wrong Bettors, Right Bettors, Buying numbers, Placing numbers, laying the odds, taking the odds, Any Craps, Hardway bets; is it any wonder why so many know so little about this game?

If the dice are "hot", you can win or lose a fortune in a matter of minutes, depending on how you are betting. But before you rush to the first Crap table you see, a firm understanding of the game is necessary. For, unlike in Blackjack, in Craps it is impossible to obtain an edge over the casino. No matter what bet you make, the casino will have the advantage. However, that advantage is very small on some of the wagers. So small, in fact, that Craps is one of the few games I actually recommend that you play.

The game is played on a large table normally covered with green felt, with each betting option clearly marked by yellow or white lettering and boundaries (see Figure 1). The layout will vary from casino to casino, but once you familiarize yourself with one layout, all are quite easy to understand.

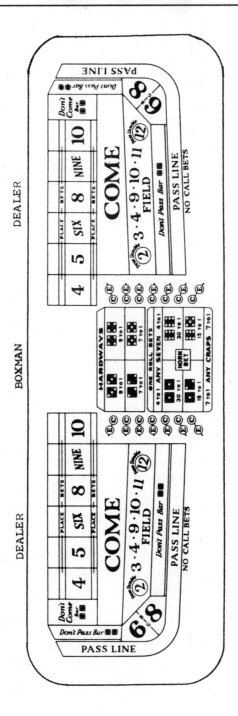

FIGURE 1

Two dealers, a stickman, and a boxman supervise the action. The dealers settle the bets, assist the players in making proper wagers and, in general, do an incredible job of keeping track of the action. The stickman assists the dealers, controls both the dice and the center table bets, and keeps up a constant chatter to enliven the game. The two dealers and the stickman rotate their positions, each working the stick and both ends of the table. The boxman is the person sitting behind the table who looks like he is guarding the casino's chips; in fact, one of his responsibilities *is* to safeguard the casino's money. In addition, the boxman watches the game to ensure proper payoffs, keeps a sharp eye on the dice, and is constantly on guard for cheats or collusion between dealers and players.

Two dice are used, each with six sides marked with from one to six small dots. When the two dice are rolled, there are 36 possible outcomes (totals of two dice). Before you can understand the various bets and your chances for success, you *must* understand how each number can be rolled. Study Figure 2 until you *fully* understand it.

OUTCOME	CAN BE ROLLED IN THESE COMBINATIONS OF TWO DICE
2	(1,1)
3	(1,2) (2,1)
4	(1,3) (2,2) (3,1)
5	(1,4) (2,3) (3,2) (4,1)
6	(1,5) (2,4) (3,3) (4,2) (5,1)
7	(1,6) (2,5) (3,4) (4,3) (5,2) (6,1)
8	(2,6) (3,5) (4,4) (5,3) (6,2)
9	(3,6) (4,5) (5,4) (6,3)
10	(4,6) (5,5) (6,4)
11	(5,6) (6,5)
12	(6,6)

Figure 2

Please note that Seven can be rolled in six combinations. Six and Eight can each be rolled in five ways. Five and Nine can be rolled in four ways. Four and Ten can each be rolled in only three ways, Three and Eleven in only two ways. Two and Twelve can only be rolled in one way each. The chance of any of those numbers being rolled on any given throw of the dice is depicted in Figure 3.

NUMBER	CHANCE OF BEING ROLLED
2 or 12	1 out of 36, or 2.8%
3 or 11	2 out of 36, or 5.6%
4 or 10	3 out of 36, or 8.3%
5 or 9	4 out of 36, or 11.1%
6 or 8	5 out of 36, or 13.9%
7	6 out of 36, or 16.7%

Figure 3

In order for you to comprehend the various bets and why they work the way they do, it is essential that you understand Figures 2 and 3. But before I describe all the betting options, let me cover the basic procedures of play. As I did with Blackjack, I will assume that you are approaching a Craps table for the first time.

Strolling through the casino early one morning, you see a Craps table being opened. No one is playing there yet, so you decide this is an opportune time to finally master this game. You station yourself next to the stickman and purchase chips from the dealer on your end of the table. You do this by simply dropping your money on the felt, preferably on a spot which is not designated as a bet. You cannot hand your money to the dealer; you must lay it down. You're hoping that no one else tries to play at the table so you can learn the game slowly, but, before you can ask the dealers what you're supposed to do, thirteen other gamblers swarm around the table. Suddenly, all hell breaks loose. Players start throwing chips all over the layout, issuing instructions to the dealers like, "Eight the hard way!", "Any Craps!", "Place the numbers!", "Gimme the Big Six!", etc. The stickman suggests, "Cover the field!", or "Bet the line!" Then he calls, "New shooter comin' out!", pushes five or more dice in front of you, and then looks at you as if you're supposed to do something. You sense a slight tingling in your stomach, feel foolish for an instant, and almost decide to leave the table because you don't have any idea what's happening. At least that's what happened to *me* the first time I played Craps.

Here's what you do: First, you must place a bet. It can be either on the Pass Line or the Don't Pass, but you must make a bet before you can throw the dice. If you don't care to roll the little cubes, simply tell the stickman and he'll pass the dice to the first person on your left. If you're not going to roll the dice, you needn't place a bet. But, for this example, I'll assume that you want to roll the dice. Next, you select two of the dice which the stickman has pushed in front of you. It doesn't make any difference which two you pick out. If you want to look like an experienced shooter (person rolling the dice), try to look calm as you toss the two dice as if you've been doing it all you life. Or, you can hold the dice in your hands for a moment, shake them, blow on them, and give them directions as to what outcome you'd like, such as "Come on, Seven!" Whatever you do to the dice prior to your throw, keep them over the table. Failure to do so will draw an immediate reprimand from one of the crew. Also, handle them with one hand only.

Okay, now you have the two dice in your hand. Your next step is to throw them hard enough that they travel the length of the felt and impact the far side of the table. This is important. If you don't hit the far end of the table on your first throw, the stickman will probably tell you to do so on your next. This is because the casino wants a "true" roll, which can only be accomplished when the dice bounce off the padded end wall of the table. Knowing this, you now heave the dice so hard that they fly over the end of the table, ricochet off the back of a pit boss, and skitter across the floor. If this happens, don't fret. The stickman will simply pass you more dice and let you start over again.

After a Point is established, you may need to roll the dice many times before obtaining either the Point or a Seven. During all those rolls, chips will be flying, people will be screaming their ecstasy or dread, and it may seem as though mass confusion reigns. Do not be concerned. Simply keep rolling the dice until the stickman pushes them in front of someone else. And, above all, do not hesitate to ask the dealer any questions which pop into your beleaguered mind. The dealers are there to help!

You continue to roll either Come-out rolls or Point rolls until you lose your bet. The dice are then passed clockwise around the table to the next shooter. You may then either leave the table or make additional bets. It is up to you.

In the following sections a short description is given for each bet available in Craps. If you don't understand the bet after your first reading, don't feel stupid. *Keep reading until you do understand*!! After several readings, you will find that there is no great mystique to this game, and, once you understand the bets, this is an easy game to play.

PASS LINE

Please note in Figure 1 that this bet covers a large portion of the Craps layout. This is one of the most popular bets and one of the easiest to understand. A Pass Line bet should be made *only* before a Come-out roll. That's important to remember. If you approach a table and do not know whether the shooter is making Come-out or Point rolls, look for a large white disc which will be placed on one of the numbers Four, Five, Six, Eight, Nine, or Ten on the layout. If the disc is on any of those numbers, the next roll is *not* a Come-out roll. The disc indicates a Point has already been established and any subsequent rolls will be Point rolls. So, if the white disc is on one of the numbers, you must wait to make a Pass Line bet until the shooter either makes the Point or passes the dice to the next shooter.

To make this wager, simply place your chips anywhere within the Pass Line boundaries. Your wager will be won or lost in the following manner:

1) If the shooter throws a Seven or Eleven on the Come-out roll, you win. The payoff is even money; for example, a $5 bet wins $5.

2) If the shooter throws a Two, a Three, or a Twelve on the Come-out roll, you lose.

3) If the shooter throws a Four, a Five, a Six, an Eight, a Nine, or a Ten on the Come-out roll, you have a Point. Then, if the shooter rolls your Point *before* rolling a Seven, you win even money. If the shooter rolls a Seven before rolling your Point, you lose.

Example: The Come-out roll is an Eight. Your bet remains on the Pass Line. The shooter then rolls a Four, a Three, an Eleven, a Nine, a Six and another Six. None of those rolls have any effect on your bet! Only Seven or Eight (the Point) can make you a winner or loser. The shooter then throws a Three, a Two, an Eleven, and an Eight. Congratulations. You just won because the shooter rolled your Point (Eight) before rolling a Seven.

When betting the Pass Line you are essentially wagering on the shooter, betting that the shooter will either throw a Seven or an Eleven on the Come-out or make the Point. People who bet on the shooter are termed "Right" bettors.

To analyze this wager, or any others, refer to Figures 2 and 3. Seven can be rolled in six ways, Eleven can be rolled in two ways; Two, Three, and Twelve can be rolled in a total of four ways. On the Come-out roll, eight combinations (outcomes) can win for you, and four will cause a loss; consequently, the odds are in your favor on the Come-out.

However, if a Point is established, you lose the advantage. Regardless of what Point is established, there is a greater chance of Seven being rolled than any other number.

To summarize, on the Come-out roll you have a 22.2% chance of winning, an 11.1% chance of losing. After a Point is established you have an 8-14% chance of winning, a 16.7% chance of losing.

Note: For the rest of the betting options, I'll let you figure out your chances of winning and losing, using the same procedure used here. Figures 2 and 3 contain all the information you need to do this.

DON'T PASS

With one slight exception, this bet is the exact opposite of a Pass Line bet. The rules governing winning or losing are reversed, for now you are betting *against* the shooter. People who bet against the shooter are termed "Wrong" bettors.

This wager can be made only *before* a Come-out roll. Place your chips in the Don't Pass section of the layout and wait for the dice to determine your fate.

1) If the shooter throws a Seven or an Eleven on the Come-out, you lose.
2) If the shooter throws a Two or a Three on the Come-out, you win even money; for example, $5 wagered wins $5.
3) Here's the small twist. Note, in Figure 1, the Bar Twelve symbols in the Don't Pass section. If the shooter throws a Twelve on the Come-out, you tie. On some tables, a roll of either Two or Three may tie instead of Twelve, but on most tables Twelve ties. In any case, the symbols in the Don't Pass section of the layout will tell you which number ties.
4) If the shooter throws a Four, a Five, a Six, an Eight, a Nine, or a Ten, you have a Point. If the shooter rolls the Point before a Seven, you lose. Should the shooter roll a Seven before the Point, you win even money.

On the Come-out roll your chance for success is only 8.3%, your chance of losing 22.2%. But if a Point is established your chance of winning improves to 16.7%, and your chance of losing drops to 8-14%, which gives you the advantage.

COME BET

This wager, with one exception, is *identical* to a Pass Line bet. The lone difference is that a Pass Line bet is made *before* a Come-out roll, while a Come bet is made only *after* a Come-out roll. If a Point has already been established when you arrive at the Crap table, and you don't want to wait for the next Come-out roll, you can make a Come bet. Again, you are betting on the shooter. Place your chips in the Come area of the layout and wait for the next throw of the dice.

1) If the shooter's very next roll is Seven or Eleven, you win even money.
2) If the shooter's very next roll is Two, Three, or Twelve, you lose.
3) Any other outcome establishes a Point for your Come bet.

Note: The Point for your Come bet may be different from the Point established on the original Come-out.

Example: I'll start at the beginning. On the Come-out roll the shooter throws a Six, so Six is the Point for the Pass Line bets. Now you approach the table and bet Come. The shooter's very next roll is an Eight, so Eight is the Point for your Come bet. Had the shooter rolled another Six, then Six would have been the Point for your Come bet. But don't let all these numbers confuse you. Your Point is determined by the first roll of the dice after you make your Come bet. That's all you must remember. In fact, you don't even have to remember it. As soon as the Point is established for your Come bet the dealer will move your chips from the Come section to your Point number. Just watch your money. At any rate, if a Point is established for your Come bet:

4) You win even money if the shooter rolls your Come Point before a Seven. If the shooter rolls a Seven first, you lose.

The percentages for winning or losing a Come bet are exactly the same as for a Pass Line bet.

DON'T COME

That's right, a Don't Come bet is nearly the exact opposite of a Come bet. A Don't Come bet is also exactly the same as a Don't Pass bet, with one exception; a Don't Pass bet can be made only *before* a Come-out roll, while a Don't Come bet can be made only *after* a Come-out roll. You are betting against the shooter.

Place your chips in the Don't Come section, then win or lose in the following manner:

1) If the shooter throws a Seven or an Eleven on the very next roll, you lose.
2) If the shooter throws a Two or a Three on the very next roll, you win even money.
3) Here's the same twist as with the Don't Pass wager. If the shooter rolls a Twelve, you tie.
4) Any other outcome is your Don't Come Point. If a Seven is then rolled before your Don't Come Point, you win even money. If the Don't Come Point is rolled first, you lose.

As soon as the Point for your Don't Come bet is established, the dealer will move your chips from the Don't Come section to the box just above your Don't Come Point. Again, watch your money. There may be several bets in that little box, and you want to make sure you know which is yours.

The percentages for this wager are identical to those for a Don't Pass bet.

Now, just in case you're confused, let's recap these first four bets. Pass Line and Come bets are won and lost in exactly the same manner. The only difference between the two is that a Come bet can be made only *after* a Come-out roll, while a Pass Line bet can be made only *before* a Come-out roll.

Don't Pass and Don't Come bets are won and lost in exactly the same manner. The only difference between the two is that a Don't Come wager can be made only *after* a Come-out roll, while a Don't Pass bet can be made only *before* a Come-out roll.

With only these four options, you can play Craps all day. If shooters are making numerous passes (rolling Sevens or Elevens on the Come-out, or making their Points) you should bet Pass or Come. When shooters are not making passes, you should bet Don't Pass or Don't Come. When shooters are making their first point and then crapping out, or the dice are not running either hot or cold, you're playing the wrong game. All four of these wagers are even money payoffs, all have the same overall advantage for the casino, approximately 1.4%. As far as the casino's advantage is concerned, these four bets are the best ones for the player.

ODDS BETS (ALSO CALLED "FREE ODDS")

When you bet Pass Line, Don't Pass, Come or Don't Come, you are allowed to make a corresponding Odds bet after the shooter establishes a Point. With Pass Line and Come, you are *taking* the odds on the shooter making the Point. With Don't Pass and Don't Come you are *laying* the odds against the shooter making the Point. These odds are also called Free Odds because the payoffs are exactly correct; the casino holds no advantage over the player. Unbelievable but true.

If you study Figure 1 you will not find an area in which to make Odds bets for the very simple reason that there is none. Because of this fact, many players are not aware that these bets are available. By taking or laying these odds the player reduces the casino's advantage on Pass Line, Don't Pass, Come, and Don't Come from 1.4% to .8%.

Odds bets are excellent wagers for the player. You run the risk of losing faster because of the additional wager, but you can also increase your winnings. I'll explain them one at a time.

PASS LINE ODDS BET

First you must make a wager on the Pass Line. Then, if a Point is rolled, you can back up your Pass Line bet by taking the odds on the Point. The exact amount of this wager depends on the casino's guidelines, but you can normally bet at least as much as your original wager on the Pass Line. To make this bet, place your additional chips an inch or two behind your original Pass Line bet. Just make sure the additional chips are outside of the Pass Line betting area outlined in Figure 1. Both your Pass Line bet and the Odds bet then lose if a Seven is rolled before the Point, win if the Point is rolled before a Seven. The Pass Line bet still pays even money, but the associated Odds bet pays in the following manner:

1) If the Point is Four or Ten, you are paid two to one. A bet of $5 would pay you $10.
2) If the Point is Five or Nine, you are paid three to two. A wager of $6 would pay you $9.
3) If the Point is Six or Eight, you are paid six to five. A wager of $5 would pay you $6.

Because of these payoffs, you must take care to always wager the correct amount to receive the correct payoffs. When in doubt, ask the dealer. Note that an Odds bet of $5 for the Four, Ten, Six or Eight could be paid correctly, but a $5 bet on Five or Nine would produce an uneven payoff ($7.50). On uneven payoffs the casino will round down to the next lowest even payoff. So a $5 bet on Five or Nine would only pay $7. This is because the lowest value chip used by most casinos is worth $1. They will not give change of fifty cents or twenty-five cents. Therefore, a bet on Five or Nine should be made in multiples of $2; bets on Six or Eight should be made in multiples of $5.

Example: You bet $10 on the Pass Line. The shooter rolls an Eight, which becomes your Point. You then place an additional $10 behind your Pass Line wager. The shooter then throws a Four, a Five, A Six, a Nine, an Eleven, another Eleven, a Two, and a Three. None of those numbers mean anything to you. The only outcomes which affect your bets are Seven and Eight. If Seven is rolled before Eight, you lose both the Pass Line bet and the Odds bet. If Eight is rolled before Seven, you win both the Pass Line bet and the Odds bet. In this example, you could lose $20 or win $22. If the Point had been Four or Ten you could have lost $20 or won $30. Had the Point been Five or Nine, you could have lost $20 or won $25.

The reason the payoffs are different for the various Point numbers is that some are more difficult to throw than others (see Figures 2 and 3).

COME BET-ODDS BET

Are you a step ahead of me by this time? Yes, Come bets-Odds bets are identical to Pass Line Odds bets. They are made in the same manner, they win or lose in the same manner, they have the same payoffs. Here are the only differences:

1) As stated earlier, your Come bet can be made only after a Come-out roll.
2) Instead of laying your Odds bet on the table, you drop your chips in front of the dealer and say, "Odds on my Come Point." If your Come Point (for example) was Eight, you would say, "Come Odds on my Eight." The dealer will then place your Odds bet on top of and slightly out of line with your Come bet.

DON'T PASS-ODDS BETS

First you must make a wager on Don't Pass. Then, if a Point is rolled, you can back up your Don't Pass bet by laying the odds on the Point. Since you are laying, rather than taking the odds, the payoffs are reversed.

1) If the Point is Four or Ten, the payoff is one to two. A $6 wager would pay $3.

2) If the Point is Five or Nine, the payoff is two to three. A $6 wager would pay $4.

3) If the Point is Six or Eight, the payoff is five to six. A $6 wager would pay $5.

Please note that this bet should be made in multiples of $6 to ensure proper payoffs.

To make this bet, place your chips for the Odds bet immediately adjacent to your Don't Pass bet, or on top of your Don't Pass bet at a slight offset. If you do it wrong, the dealer will show you how.

If the Point is rolled before a Seven, you lose both your Don't Pass and Odds bets. If a Seven is rolled before the Point, you win both your Don't Pass and Odds bets.

DON'T COME-ODDS BETS

Right again. Don't Come-Odds bets are identical to Don't Pass-Odds bets. They are made in the same manner, they win or lose in the same manner, they have the same payoffs. Here are the only differences:

1) As stated earlier, your Don't Come bet can be made only *after* a Come-out roll.

2) Instead of placing your Odds bet on the table, you drop your chips in front of the dealer and say, "Odds on my Don't Come", or "Odds on my Don't Four," or words to that effect. The dealer will then place your Odds bet in the Don't Come section of the box just above your Don't Come Point.

Again, the overall casino advantage on Pass Line, Don't Pass, Come, or Don't Come is about 1.4%. If you take or lay the corresponding Odds bets, the casino advantage is reduced to about .8%.

Knowing only what we have covered so far, you can play craps right alongside all the heavy hitters. The easiest way to become accustomed to craps is to keep it simple, especially when you are learning. Walk up to a table, buy chips, and put $2 (or the table minimum) on the Pass Line before the next Come-out roll. You will win or lose as described earlier. Should you win, bet another $2. If you lose, bet another $2. But stay with that simple Pass Line wager the entire time you are at the table. All hell may be breaking loose, with players shouting all kinds of directions to the dealers, tossing chips everywhere, and pleading for their numbers to be rolled. Some of the players may be wagering thousands of dollars. But none of that means anything to you. All you have to do is watch your Pass Line wager and let the dice decide your fate.

Once you are more comfortable with the game, try the Pass Line and then take the Odds. If you become bored with having only one bet on the table, bet Pass, then Come. That could give you two numbers. In fact, one of the most popular betting strategies you will see being used at the tables is to bet Pass, Come, and Come. Yes, that could give you three different numbers. Just think about it. You bet Pass. The shooter rolls a Four. You bet Come. The shooter rolls a Five. So now Four is the point for your Pass bet, and Five is the point for your Come bet. You bet Come again. The shooter rolls a Six. Now you're got three numbers working for you with three separate bets. And that's wonderful so long as that shooter keeps throwing numbers. But if the shooter all of a sudden rolls a seven, you lose all three wagers.

Don't Pass and Don't Come can be worked in the same manner.

You could actually stop reading this chapter right now and play craps as well as anyone. The odds against you on these first four betting options are about as low as you're going to find anywhere in the casino, so don't hesitate to try them. However, there are many other wagers waiting for your chips, so let's investigate them.

PLACE BETS

These bets can only be made on the numbers Four, Five, Six, Eight, Nine or Ten. Do not make this bet yourself! Drop your chips in front of the dealer and tell him what numbers you want to place. You may place any or all of the numbers, you may make or remove this bet at any time. When you want to remove your bet, tell the dealer "Off my Place bets", or "My Place bets are off".

See if you can follow the intent of this rule: Unless the player makes a request for the Place bets to be off, they are always on for all rolls except the Come-out roll, when they are always off unless requested to be on. Sound confusing? To clarify matters, it is to your advantage for

Place bets to be on at all times. Whether you win or lose a Place bet is determined in the following matter:

1) If a Seven is rolled before your Place number, you lose.
2) If your Place number is rolled before a Seven, you win.

Here are the payoffs:

>Four and Ten pay nine to five
>Five and Nine pay seven to five
>Six and Eight pay seven to six

Please note that these payoffs are less than those for Free Odds bets associated with Pass, Don't Pass, Come and Don't Come. Not a lot less, but enough to increase the casino's advantage. On Four and Ten the casino's advantage is about 6.7%. For Five and Nine it is 4%. For Six and Eight it is only about 1.5%, which makes Six and Eight the best numbers to place.

Placing numbers is another simple and effective way to play craps. Walk up to the table. Lay your chips in front of the dealer and say "Place the Six, please." You don't care what the point is. All you need concern yourself with is whether that Six shows up before a Seven. Want more excitement? Place both the Six and Eight. Got a hot shooter? Place the Six, the Eight, the Five and Nine. Has the shooter tossed your numbers a few times? Double up on your bets.

I can't emphasize this enough: Pass, Don't Pass, Come, Don't Come, taking or laying the Free Odds and Placing numbers. These are by far the best bets at the craps table. And if you are serious about winning money you must play only those games and make only those bets which have the smallest edge against you. A long-winded sentence, but worth remembering. This is part of becoming Gambling Smart. Yes, there are still more betting options, but, quite frankly, unless you are going to become *very* serious about craps don't even attempt to learn all of them at this time. I will explain'em, but that doesn't mean you gotta try'em.

BUY BETS

Buy bets are very similar to Place bets. As with Place bets, you are essentially wagering that the shooter will roll your number before a

Seven. Buy bets can be made or removed at any time, they are made on the same numbers as Place bets, and you make the bet by dropping your chips in front of the dealer. But now you say, "Buy the Eight", or "Buy the Four". The similarities end with the above. Here are the differences:

1) A small marker, which looks as if it came from a tiddlywinks game, is set on top of your chips to distinguish your Buy bet from a Place bet. The marker has "Buy" stamped on it.
2) The payoffs are different:

> Four and Ten pay two to one
> Five and Nine pay three to two
> Six and Eight pay six to five

3) On Buy bets the casino charges a five percent service charge in multiples of $1. If you want to bet $10, it will cost you $11. A bet of $20 would cost $21. A $40 bet would cost $42 ($40 x 5% = $2). The charge is always in multiples of $1 because the casino does not give change of fifty cents or twenty-five cents.

The casino advantage on buy bets is approximately 5%, so this is not a great bet for the player.

LAY BETS

This wager is nearly the exact opposite of a Buy bet. You are betting that the shooter will roll a Seven before your Lay number. You can make a Lay bet on the Four, Five, Six, Eight, Nine or Ten. Pass the dealer your chips and say, "Lay the odds on the Six" or "Lay the Eight". The dealer will place your chips in the Don't Come section of the number you request, then put a small Buy marker on top of them. Lay bets are always on, even on the Come-out roll. If a Seven is rolled before your number, the payoffs are:

> Four and Ten pay one to two
> Five and Nine pay two to three
> Six and Eight pay five to six

As with Buy bets, there is a five percent service charge involved, but the five percent is based on your potential winnings instead of on your bet.

Example: You want to make a $40 Lay bet on the Four. If you were to win, the payoff would be $20. Five percent of $20 is $1, which is added to the cost of your bet. So, in order to be paid correctly on a bet of $40, you need to bet $41. Sound dumb? The casino advantage on Lay bets is 2.5% on the Four and Ten, 3.2% on the Five and Nine, 4% on the Six or Eight. If you want to try a Lay bet, make it on the Four or Ten.

BIG SIX OR BIG EIGHT

This is another wager which can be made or removed at anytime. It is also another bad bet. You can make this bet yourself by placing chips in the Big Six or Big Eight portion of the table layout. Your bet is won or lost in the following manner:

1) If Six or Eight (depending on which you bet) is rolled before Seven, you win even money.
2) If Seven is thrown before Six or Eight, you lose.

Here's why this is a bad bet. Six and Eight can each be rolled in five combinations. Seven can be rolled in six combinations. The true payoff for this wager, therefore, should be six to five instead of even money. By paying even money the casino reaps an advantage of 9.09%!

Note: In Atlantic City this bet is usually paid off at seven to six, which lowers the casino advantage to 1.5%. This is much better for the player, but all bets should be made in multiples of $6.

HARD TEN OR HARD FOUR

I've lumped these two together because the payoffs and probabilities are the same for both numbers. They are two separate bets which can be made by passing chips to the *stickman*, who controls all bets in the center of the table. This bet can be made or removed at any time.

Hard Four can only be rolled one way (two, two). Hard Ten can only be rolled one way (five, five). You are betting that Hard Four or

Hard Ten (whichever you choose) will be rolled before Seven, *and* before any other combination of Four or Ten.

The payoff is seven to one, which sounds juicy. But let's say you bet the Hard Four. Only one combination can win for you (two, two). Eight combinations will lose the bet; six combinations of Seven, plus (one, three) and (three, one). The true payoff should be eight to one, but since the casino only pays seven to one its advantage is 11.1%!

HARD SIX OR HARD EIGHT

This bet is also made through the stickman; it may be placed or removed before any roll. The payoffs and probabilities are the same for both. If you make a bet on Hard Six you are wagering that (three,three) will be rolled before any Seven, *and also* before any other combination of Six. The payoff is nine to one.

But Hard Six can only be rolled in one way, while there are six combinations of Seven and four others of Six: (one,five), (two,four), (four,two), or (five,one). One way can win, ten will lose. Ditto for the Hard Eight. The true payoff for these bets should be ten to one, but since the casino only pays nine to one their advantage on this one is 9.09%.

ONE ROLL BETS

All of the following wagers are decided by one roll of the dice. After making these wagers, the very next roll will cause you to win or lose. With the lone exception of the Field bet, which you can easily place for yourself, all of these bets are made through the stickman. If you want action on each roll of the dice, here's your chance.

Field Bets

This bet is very popular because seven different outcomes (Two, Three, Four, Nine, Ten, Eleven or Twelve) can win, while only four (Five, Six, Seven or Eight) can lose. However, the winning numbers can be rolled in a total of only sixteen ways. You have a 44.4% chance of winning and a 55.6% chance of losing. That means the casino has an 11.2% advantage.

The odds improve when the casino pays two to one or three to one when a Two or a Twelve is rolled, but the odds are still stacked against you. You might get lucky for a few rolls, but over the long haul the casino edge will grind you down.

Any Seven

Here you are betting the next roll will be a Seven. Since there are six ways to roll a Seven, there are six combinations which will win for you. The other thirty possible outcomes cause you to lose. The true payoff on this bet should be five to one (thirty to six), but since the casino only pays four to one its advantage is 16.7%.

Any Craps

Now you're betting the next roll will be either Two, Three, or Twelve. Two can be rolled in one way, Three can be rolled in two ways, Twelve can be rolled in one way. Four outcomes can win for you, the other thirty-two will cause a loss. The true payoff should be eight to one, but since the casino only pays seven to one its advantage on this bet is 11.1%.

Two

Another poor wager. You are betting the next roll will be a Two. The payoff is thirty to one, which sounds very enticing.

But Two can only be rolled in one way. Only one outcome can win for you, the other thirty-five cause a loss. The true payoff should be thirty-five to one, but since the casino only pays thirty to one its advantage is a very nice (for the casino) 13.9%.

Twelve

Same as Two, above.

Three

Now you're betting the next roll will be a Three. The payoff is fifteen to one. But Three can only be rolled in two ways. Two combinations can win for you, thirty-four can lose. The true payoff should be seventeen to one, but since the casino only pays fifteen to one its advantage is 11.8%.

Eleven

Same as Three, above.

Craps-Eleven (Also Called a Horn Bet)

This one is even worse than all the others. Here you're wagering that a Two, a Three, an Eleven or a Twelve will show on the next roll. The payoffs are as follows:

> Two pays thirty to one
> Three pays fifteen to one
> Twelve pays thirty to one

Since you're covering four numbers, you must bet four chips. From our earlier discussions, you already know that the payoffs for all these numbers are incorrect, giving the casino an advantage of from 11.8% to 13.9%. In addition, even if you won on one of the numbers, you still lose your other three chips, which makes the casino advantage even higher. If you like these kinds of odds, perhaps you should try Russian Roulette.

DOUBLE AND TRIPLE ODDS

I am referring to the Odds bets which can be made in conjunction with Pass Line, Come, Don't Pass, and Don't Come wagers. Many casinos allow these Odds bets to be made in double or triple the amount of your initial wager. And there are even a handful who will allow you to go as high as ten times odds.

Example: You are playing at a table which offers Double Odds. Your Pass Line bet is $10. A Point is established. You may now wager up to $20 on the associated Odds bet. If you were playing at a Triple Odds table, your Pass Line Odds bet could be as high as $30.

Both Double and Triple Odds reduce the casino's advantage, but don't get carried away. One bad spell of luck at a Double or Triple Odds table will quickly demolish your gambling stake.

WAGERING LIMITS

Minimum wagers at most Crap tables will be either $2 or $5, with the maximum running up to $2,000 or $3,000. I suggest that you start at a $2 table until you gain confidence. Then, if you want more action, most casinos will allow you to make an Odds bet which is greater than your original Pass Line, Come, Don't Pass or Don't Come bet.

Example: If your original wager is three dollars, your associated Odds bet can be four dollars if the Point is Five or Nine, five dollars if the Point is Six or Eight. This is a good proposition for the player, and also allows the casino to make correct payoffs.

All this can be very confusing, so make certain you know the exact bets allowed by the casino. For most of us, it is difficult to remember betting units, payoffs, and how to make the proper bets to ensure accurate payoffs without becoming bewildered.

MONEY MANAGEMENT

After reading this chapter you should have enough knowledge to play Craps with confidence. But, as I also mentioned when discussing Blackjack, none of your knowledge of Craps means anything unless you manage your money properly. You can make all the right bets and still lose money. To help prevent severe losses, I offer the following suggestions:

1) Start with at least 50 units. 75 units would be more practical.
2) Change tables if you lose 10% of your stake. A new table can provide you with fresh enthusiasm. If your casino only has one or two Crap tables open, then change casinos.
3) If you win as many as 10 units at any table, *do not* lose it back! As soon as you start winning, put your original chips in your pocket and play with your winnings, then leave the table before the casino can recapture its losses.
4) If you win as many as 20 units, double your unit. If you win another 20 units, double your unit again.
5) Make only the wagers on which the casino has the lowest advantage. These include: Pass Line and Odds, Don't Pass and Odds, Come bets and Odds, Don't Come and Odds, Placing the Six or Eight.

6) Regardless of whether you bet Pass Line, Come, Don't Pass or Don't Come, always take or lay the associated Odds bets, if you can afford it. While this can cause you to lose twice as fast, you can also win more and reduce the casino's edge from 1.4% to .8%.

7) Do not switch your bets back and forth in an attempt to catch a good or bad run of the dice. If you are betting the Pass Line, stay with it. If you are betting Don't Come, stay with it. If you switch back and forth you may get caught between flip-flopping dice and lose every bet. Most good gamblers follow this rule and find it reduces frustration.

8) Do not double your bet after a loss. If you lose six or seven consecutive bets, which is entirely possible, you will blow your whole gambling stake.

9) Develop a game plan before you start betting. Know *how* you want to bet, *what* you want to bet, and the payoffs. Stick to those basic wagers until your knowledge is complete. Then, and only then, should you experiment with any exotic bets. Probably the greatest difficulty in playing Craps is that with so much action taking place, with so many people screaming, with so many chips flying around, it is very easy to become confused. Do not rush yourself! You do not have to place a bet on every roll of the dice. If you make a mistake on a bet, such as placing your chips in the wrong area, the casino will not show you any sympathy.

10) Whenever you are in doubt, seek the assistance of the dealers. It is their job to assist you. There is no such thing as a stupid question. In fact, it is in your best interest to develop a rapport with the dealers. Treat them with respect and you'll receive all the help you need.

That's all for this chapter, but don't forget to read and study the practical advice at the end of this book, which includes a suggestion on betting strategy.

Chapter 3

Baccarat

If you are a person who desires the simplest of card games, Baccarat is for you. There are only three player options:

1) You can bet on the Banker's hand.
2) You can bet on the Player's hand.
3) You can bet on Tie.

And since a bet on Tie is a foolish wager, you can narrow down the options to just two: bet on Players or Bankers. Yes, the game really is that simple.

Yet, even though Baccarat is easy to play, most people assume you need to be a millionaire and have superior intelligence in order to sit at a Baccarat table. Not so, not so. All you need is money.

Most every casino has at least one Baccarat table, with the betting limits ranging from $20 to $10,000 or more. Perhaps a minimum wager of $20 scares a lot of people away from the game. I'm sure it does. But if you can afford to wager $20 on each round of play, Baccarat offers very little disadvantage to the player, with the casino's advantage ranging from only 1.2% to about 1.4%. So let's take a good look at this game.

Trudging through the casino one evening you note that one gaming area is situated off to the side of the room, either partitioned or roped off from the rest of the gambling areas, making the activities in that room seem very private. Upon closer inspection you see men in tuxedos, beautiful women in evening dresses, posh decorations. It looks glamorous, exotic, mysterious. There's even a man in a chair perched high above the action. Other spectators grouped near you are trying to watch the play, a look of awe in their eyes. But, being slightly different from the majority, you are not satisfied with watching. Even though you're dressed in denims and a cowboy shirt, you hold your head erect, jut out your chin and march into that room as if you owned the casino. A few of the gamblers sitting at the table glance at you with expressionless faces as you confidently sit in the first available chair.

As with all other casino games, your first step is to purchase chips. Then, before making any wagers, you study the table layout (see Figure 1).

Assume you're at seat number 1. Note that there are only three compartments where you can place a wager, all of which are within easy reach directly in front of your position. Two of the casino employees (dealers), both sitting on the same side of the table, are shuffling eight decks of cards. For the moment, there is nothing for you to do. You can lean back in your comfortable chair and relax.

After a short time the dealers are finished shuffling the cards and the ritual begins. One of the dealers hands you a plain plastic card and moves all eight decks in your direction. Being astute, you quickly determine that he wants you to cut the cards. You insert the plastic card into the decks, the dealer cuts the cards at that point and then places all eight decks into a plastic shoe similar to those at the Blackjack tables. So far, so good. The other players assume that you know what you're doing.

Next, the dealer removes the first card from the shoe and shows it to the players. It is a Six. You say, "Big deal", with sarcasm filling your voice. Ah, you just labeled yourself as a novice. The dealer frowns at your ignorance of Baccarat custom and then removes six more cards from the shoe, placing them in a discard slot in the middle of the table. If the first card had been a Four, four cards would have been discarded. Had the first card been a Nine, nine cards would have been discarded. Get the picture? The numbers of cards which are "burned" is determined by the first card out of the shoe. This helps prevent cheating.

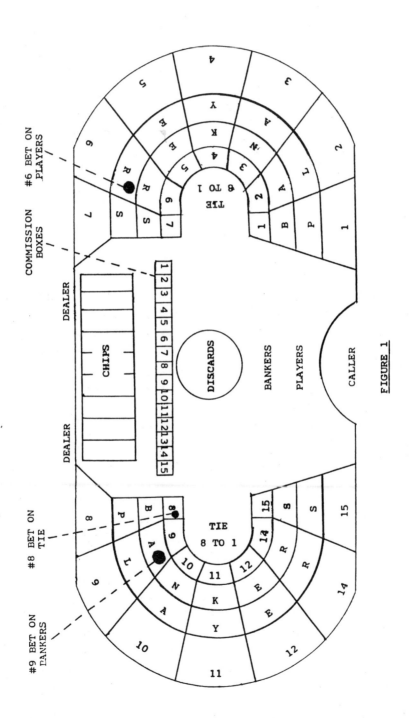

FIGURE 1

You then expect the dealer to slide the cards out to the players, but something strange happens. The dealer shoves the entire plastic shoe in front of your position. You think: "My God, what now?"

Well, you've just become the Banker. And no, that does not mean you have to pay off all the winning bets when the game starts. It simply means you're going to be the dealer for a while. Like a lot of other people, you have confused Baccarat with Chemin-de Fer because of the James Bond movie *Goldfinger*. In Baccarat the *casino* collects and pays off, not the Banker. You issue a sigh of relief. But since you're the Banker, you *must* make a bet. You can bet on Bankers or Players, but most gamblers bet on Bankers when they have the shoe. The person with the shoe is the Banker, so most Bankers bet on Bankers. Make sense? You don't have to be the Banker if you don't want to be. If you don't want to deal the cards, simply say "No thanks", or words to that effect. The shoe will then be offered to the person on your right.

Okay, you decide you want to deal, so you place the minimum wager of $20 on Bankers. For a moment, you wonder how you'll be able to deal cards to the players at the other end of the table, but another casino employee standing opposite the dealers solves the problem for you. He is the "caller", the person who directs the play of the game. He instructs you to deal him a card, then one to yourself, then another to him, then another to yourself, all face down. The first and third cards form the Player's hand, the second and fourth form the Banker's hand. Right. There are only two hands; the Banker's and the Player's.

Now more ritual. The caller passes his two cards, which form the Player's hand, to a lady sitting at the far end of the table who has $2,000 wagered on the Player's hand. The reason he gave them to her is because she had the largest bet on Players. The lady turns the cards over, face up, then passes them back to the caller, who places them face up on the table in front of him. You wonder why the caller couldn't just turn the cards over by himself, but you keep quiet.

The caller then turns to you and directs you to turn over the Banker's hand. You do so, seeing a Six and a Nine. Because of your Blackjack experience, you assume that the hand is worth a total of 15. However, being a novice, you keep your mouth shut. And it's good that you didn't say anything. For, you see, it is impossible for any hand to total more than 9. Aces are counted as one. Tens, Jacks, Queens and Kings are counted as zero. All other cards are face value; for example, a Six is worth six, a Five is worth five. If the total of the cards is a two-digit number, like 15, the first digit is dropped. So 15 becomes 5. If the total were 25, the hand would still be 5.

At the caller's request, you pass the Banker's hand to him. He places the Banker's hand on the table in front of him, just slightly above the Player's hand.

Did you win or lose? You don't know yet. The Banker's hand is 5, and assume that the Player's hand is 4. But, the way this game is played, the Player's hand may need another card, the Banker's hand may need another card, both may need another, or neither may need another. In any case, neither hand can have more than three cards. The beauty of Baccarat is that the decision as to whether either hand needs another card is not yours to make. The caller is in charge of the game. He will tell you if either hand needs another card, basing his decisions on the very strict rules which govern this game. You may request a copy of the printed rules and the casino will be happy to oblige you.

In this case the caller says to you, "A card for Players." You deal the card face down to the caller, who places it face up adjacent to the Player's hand. The Player's hand is always acted upon before the Banker's hand. The card is a Seven, increasing the Player's hand to 11, which is really only 1. But you're not done yet.

The caller tells you, "A card for Bankers." You dutifully slip another card out of the shoe, face down, and pass it to the caller. He turns it over adjacent to the Banker's other two cards. It is a Three, giving the Banker's hand a total of 18, which is really just 8. Remember? You always drop the first digit of a two-digit total.

The caller announces, "Bankers win, eight over one." The two dealers collect the losing bets on Players and pay off the winning bets on Bankers. But as the dealer on your side of the table pays off your bet on Bankers, you notice that he is also placing a little chip in a row of boxes in front of him. More specifically, he places one of those chips in the box marked 1, which is your position. Don't be alarmed. When you bet on Bankers and win, you must pay the casino a five percent commission. The dealer is simply keeping track of how much commission you owe. He will collect the commission later, before you leave the table or after the last hand is played from the shoe.

I know, a five percent commission on winnings sounds terrible. But what you don't know yet is that the rules governing the game favor the

Banker's hand. Consequently the Banker's hand wins more often than the Player's hand. Because of this, the casino must charge a commission to make any money. Had you bet on Players and won, you wouldn't have paid any commission. If you don't want to pay commissions, just bet on Players all the time. But, as I stated, Bankers wins more often than Players.

Now, does that sound like a difficult game? Of course not. The most difficult part was being the Banker (dealer), and all you had to do was follow the caller's instructions. Had you not been the Banker, you would have simply placed a bet, relaxed, and awaited the outcome.

Let's take this example a step further. You deal another hand in the same manner as the first. But this time Player's wins. All that happens is that you pass the shoe to the person on your right. The shoe changes whenever the Banker's hand loses, and travels around the table counterclockwise. It keeps moving until the plain plastic card shows up . . .the same plastic card you inserted into the decks at the beginning. That hand is played out to completion, then the decks are either reshuffled or eight new decks are introduced.

Assume that you bet on Bankers sixteen times and won fourteen times. You bet $20 on each hand. Now it's time to pay your commission. $20 x 14 winning hands = $280. 5% of $280 = $14. Is that so terrible? Of course not, especially since the rules favor Bankers.

The chart depicted below shows the rules administered by the caller, but you needn't memorize them. You have no control, anyway. You simply bet on Bankers or Players and either win or lose. While it's possible for the caller to make a mistake, that possibility is very remote.

PLAYER'S RULES

If Player's Two-Card Total Is	Player Must
0, 1, 2, 3, 4, 5	DRAW
6, 7	STAND
8, 9	NATURAL**

**A Natural is an automatic winner unless the Banker's two-card total is also 8 or 9, in which case a tie could be the result.

Figure 2

BANKER'S RULES

Banker's Two-Card Total	Draws Card If Player Draws A	Does Not Draw If Player Draws A
0, 1, 2	MUST DRAW	MUST DRAW
3	0,1,2,3,4,5,6,7,9	8
4	2,3,4,5,6,7	0,1,8,9
5	4,5,6,7	0,1,2,3,8,9
6	6,7	0,1,2,3,4,5,8,9
7	MUST STAND	MUST STAND
8,9	NATURAL**	NATURAL**

**A natural is an automatic winner unless the Player's hand is also a natural.

Figure 3

The idea of the game is to get a total of 9, or as close to 9 as possible. Whichever hand is closer to 9 is the winner. If either hand is dealt 8 or 9 on the first two cards, that hand has a Natural. If one hand has a Natural and the other doesn't, the Natural wins automatically. If one has 8, the other 9, the 9 wins the hand. Once a Natural is revealed, that round is over.

Now let's look at a few sample hands.

Example #1. Players is dealt a Queen and a Ten. Bankers is dealt a Two and a Three. What happens now? Well, refer to the rules. The Player's total is 0, so Players must draw another card. Say that Players receives a Six, for a total of 6. And since Players drew a Six, Bankers must also take an additional card. Say that Bankers draws a Seven, for a total of 12, which is really just 2, and loses the round. The caller says, "Players wins, six over two."

Example #2. Players receives a Six and a Five. Bankers receives a Ten and a Seven. What happens next? Again, refer to the rules. If the Player's total is 1, Players must draw a card. But what does Bankers do with a total of 7? Well, if Bankers has a total of 7, it does not make any difference what card Players draws. Bankers *must* stand on 7. Even if Players draws an Eight, for a total of 9, Bankers still can't draw another card. Yes, even though it means Bankers will lose the round.

Example #3. Player's total is 4. Banker's total is 4. Players must draw a card, does, and receives a Three for a total of 7. And since Players drew a Three, Bankers must draw a card also.

Example 4. Again, Players and Bankers each have a total of 4. But this time the Player's hand draws a Queen, and therefore does not improve its total. Can Bankers now take another card? No. The round would end in a tie.

Example #5. Player's hand receives a King and a Jack. Banker's hand catches an Ace and a Ten. Player's hand totals 20, which is really just 0. Banker's hand totals 11, which is really just 1. Players must draw an additional card, does, and receives another Jack. Player's hand is still worth only 0. You've bet on Bankers, so you think you've won the hand, 1 over 0. But, alas, any time the Banker's hand has a total of 0, 1, or 2 Bankers must draw a card. In this example, Bankers could possibly turn a winning hand into a losing hand by taking an additional card, but that's the rules, folks.

Now the next time you have an extra $100 in your pocket you can bounce into the Baccarat area and make at least five bets. You can sit there and sip your drink, cast looks of disdain at the spectators on the other side of the ropes, and feel like a high roller. What the hell? Go ahead and do it at least once in your life.

Remember how simple it is. You bet on Bankers or Players. It's really that easy. Who knows? You might get lucky. Baccarat attracts many wealthy gamblers, so you can bet the minimum and watch the high rollers win or lose hundreds of thousands of dollars. Recent reports indicate that some casinos generate as much as one third of their total income from Baccarat. Next time, instead of marveling at what is happening in that small private room, join the action.

The best thing about this game is that it is entirely possible to win more than you lose, even if you play the five percent commission. The casino's advantage on Players is about 1.4%. On Bankers (including the commission), the casino's advantage is only 1.2%, which makes a bet on Bankers one of the best wagers in the casino.

Oh, yes. I forgot to tell you. That person hovering over the game from his tall, tall chair is called the ladderman. It is his job to oversee the game and watch for cheating and collusion between dealers and players. Unless you're trying to cheat, ignore him.

MINI-BACCARAT

As the term implies, Mini-Baccarat is a smaller version of the same game, It is played at a smaller table (normally found near the Blackjack tables), allows a smaller minimum wager ($2-$5), and one dealer does everything: the dealing, the exchanging of chips on wins or losses, the calling of the hands.

There are not many of these tables available, but they are a good place to start if you can find one. Play Mini-Baccarat until you gain confidence, then move on to the big table.

However, exercise some care. In Baccarat, as played on the big tables, you don't lose ties. If you bet on either Bankers or Players and the result is a tie, you don't win or lose unless you have bet on Tie. But in quite a few of the Mini-Baccarat games the casino wins all ties. This rule is bad for gamblers, so watch out for it.

Also, the minimum commission charged on a winning wager on Bankers is usually twenty-five cents. So even if you wagered only two dollars, which should mean a commission of ten cents, you still must pay twenty-five cents. Not much difference, but those nickels and dimes add up in a hurry.

MONEY MANAGEMENT

Due to the larger minimum wager required for this game, I suggest that there are only two times when you should play Baccarat:

1) If you have at least $100 fun money to blow.
2) If you purchase additional books on Baccarat systems and can play with a bankroll of at least $5,000.

Note: In Atlantic City you may have difficulty finding a $20 game. In an effort to make Baccarat even more exclusive, the casinos in Atlantic City often require a minimum wager of $40, $60 or more, with a frequent minimum of $100.

Chapter 4

Roulette

Who would have thought that a large wheel and small ball could cause the loss of millions of dollars? Defined in most dictionaries as a gambling game in which players bet on which compartment of a revolving wheel a small ball will come to rest in, the game is easy to learn, easy to play.

A dealer (croupier) oversees the betting, makes payoffs, rotates the wheel and spins the ivory ball. If the ball drops into the compartment housing one of the numbers that you've bet, you win. There is no mystique to this game. The wheel rotates, the ball spins, you win or lose.

I have not supplied a diagram of a Roulette wheel since a few moments' observation of one can tell you all you need to know. The only difference between Roulette wheels is that some have only 0 and others have 0 *and* 00. However, unless you leave the United States, all wheels will have both 0 and 00. All wheels in the world also have the numbers 1-36, eighteen of which are red, eighteen of which are black; 0 and 00 normally have a green background. The red numbers are 1, 3, 5, 7, 9, 12, 14, 16, 18, 19, 21, 23, 25, 27, 30, 32, 34 and 36. The black numbers are 2, 4, 6, 8, 10, 11, 13, 15, 17, 20, 22, 24, 26, 28, 29, 31, 33 and 35. Consequently, there are 38 compartments on each American wheel.

According to the law of averages, each number should come up once every 38 spins. Unfortunately, the wheel and ball do not understand the law of averages.

I once spent an entire evening noting the results of each spin at a Roulette table. I did not make any wagers. I simply jotted down the outcomes of each spin. Mentally, I was betting on number 32, but I did not actually extend a wager. Good thing, too. For had I actually been betting on number 32, I would have lost money. Number 32 was the result on the fifth spin after I arrived at the table, but it did not repeat again until the 147th spin of the wheel. Had I been wagering real money, I would have bet 147 units and won back only 70. Yet during that same time period, the number 00 came up on twelve spins. Had I wagered on 00 I would have bet 147 units and won 420 units. The point is this: If the law of averages had held completely true, both 32 and 00 would have been the result about four times each. But, as I've already mentioned in other sections, the law of averages is not based on 38 spins. It is based on millions of spins. So it is possible to sit at a Roulette table all night without seeing your favorite number appear. Conversely, it is also possible to see your favorite number appear many, many times. And that's why we play this silly game, isn't it?

Figure 1
ROULETTE BETTING LAYOUT

00	3	6	9	12	15	18	21	24	27	30	33	36	2-1
	2	5	8	11	14	17	20	23	26	29	32	35	2-1
0	1	4	7	10	13	16	19	22	25	28	31	34	2-1

| 1st 12 | | | | 2nd 12 | | | | 3rd 12 | | | |
| 1-18 | | EVEN | | RED | | BLACK | | ODD | | 19-36 | |

Your first step is to purchase chips. If you already have chips from playing one of the other casino games, you can use them to make your Roulette wagers, but it is more advisable to purchase Roulette chips; in fact, you may be asked to do so. If three people each bet a red casino $5 chip and one of them wins, who does the dealer pay? How does the dealer know which chip belongs to which player? Avoid this potential problem by purchasing Roulette chips. These chips are designed especially for Roulette; each player who buys them receives a different color, and you can assign to them whatever money value you want.

Example: You are going to play at a table which requires a $2 minimum bet. You want to buy $20 in chips. Depending on the casino's rules, you might obtain (at your request) twenty $1 chips, forty chips worth fifty cents each, or eighty chips worth twenty-five cents each. The dealer may give you orange chips, purple chips or yellow chips, but whichever you receive, you will be the only person at the Roulette table with that color. And the dealer will mark your chips, so there will be no misunderstanding as to whether you are playing with chips worth fifty cents, twenty-five cents, or some other value.

Roulette chips can be used only at a Roulette table. You purchase them from the dealer, you sell them back to the dealer before you leave the table. *Do not* leave the table with the chips! If you try to take them from one table to another, they will not be honored by the new dealer, because the new dealer does not know what value your chips have been assigned.

Also, when you exit the table the dealer will not cash your Roulette chips for real money, but will provide you with regular casino chips such as those used at Blackjack and Craps.

Once you have chips, your betting options are numerous, each wager winning or losing on the very next spin of the wheel. Figure 2 (see following page) is a list of the options, along with the casino's advantage for each bet.

Actual payoffs are what you actually receive if you win. True odds indicate what the payoffs *should be.* The difference between the two is the casino's advantage. As you can see, the Five Number bet is the worst that you can place.

Figure 2

TYPE OF WAGER	ACTUAL PAYOFF	TRUE ODDS	CASINO ADVANTAGE
ONE NUMBER	35:1	37:1	5.26%
TWO NUMBERS	17:1	18:1	5.26%
THREE NUMBERS	11:1	11.7:1	5.26%
FOUR NUMBERS	8:1	8.5:1	5.26%
FIVE NUMBERS	6:1	6.6:1	7.89%
SIX NUMBERS	5:1	5.3:1	5.26%
DOZENS	2:1	2.2:1	5.26%
COLUMNS	2:1	2.2:1	5.26%
RED OR BLACK	1:1	1.1:1	5.26%
ODD OR EVEN	1:1	1.1:1	5.26%
1-18 OR 19-36	1:1	1.1:1	5.26%

INSIDE BETS

These bets can only be made in the portion of the betting layout seen in Figure 3.

Figure 3

The reason these bets are classified as Inside bets is because the maximum amount that you wager differs from what are known as Outside bets (described later). Always ask the dealer about the maximum wager when you buy your Roulette chips. Though the table may advertise a $500 maximum, this does not necessarily mean you can make a $500 bet. The amount you can wager on an Inside bet varies from casino to casino. Usually, the maximum wager on a One Number bet is $25. However, a $25 bet on a single number would pay $875. Obviously, if the casino allowed $500 wagers on single numbers, where the payoff would be $17,500, a person on a lucky streak could quickly force a closing of the table.

Also: If you are playing at a $2 table, you must make bets *totaling* $2. You do not need to bet the entire $2 on just one bet. If you were playing with chips worth fifty cents, you could make four different bets. In other words, your $2 could be spread all over the betting layout.

All the following are Inside bets:

One Number

Figure 3 shows five different One Number bets (00, 8, 13, 21 and 29). Simply make sure your chips are clearly placed within the boundaries of the number or numbers you select. Since there are 38 numbers on the betting layout, there are 38 different ways to make this bet. You can wager on as many numbers as you like.

Note: As with all other Roulette bets, it is permissible to place your chips on top of the chips of the other players. Do not be alarmed if someone stacks five blue chips atop your purple ones. If you are wagering more than one chip on a bet, stack your chips on top of each other.

Two Number Bets

Figure 4

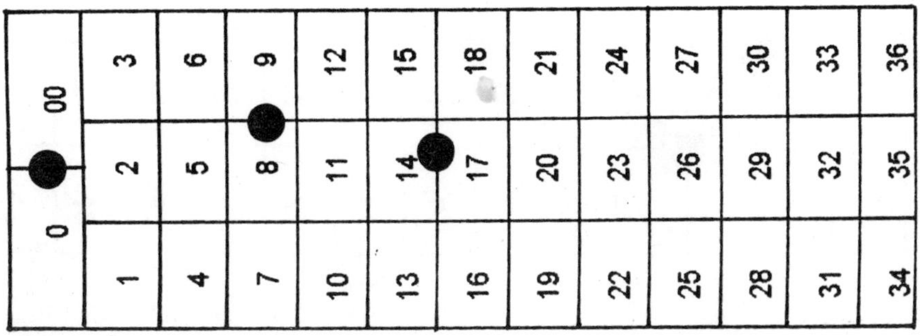

The two numbers you select must be adjacent. There are 62 different ways to place this bet. Figure 4 shows three ways (0,00 or 8,9 or
14,17). You could *not* cover numbers such as 2,16 or 23,36 since they
are not adjacent.

Three Number Bets

Figure 5

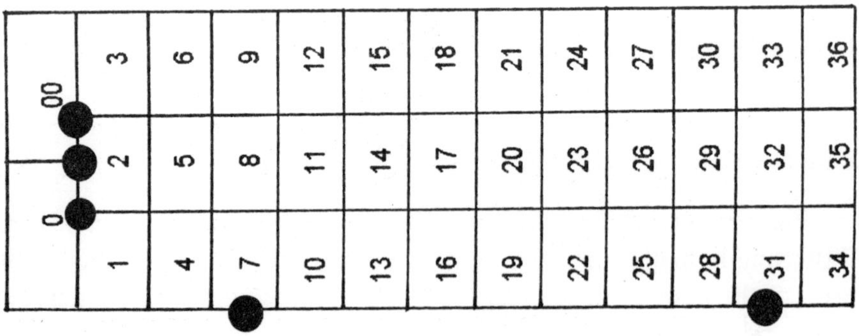

All of the bets in Figure 5 cover three numbers each (1,0,2 or 0,2,00
or 2,00,3 or 7,8,9 or 31,32,33). In all, this bet can be made in fifteen
different ways.

Four Number Bets

Figure 6

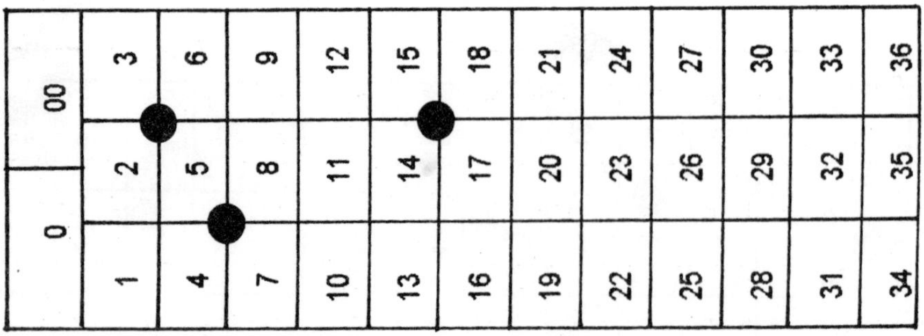

The three wagers shown in Figure 6 (2,3,5,6 or 14,15,17,18 or 4,5,7,8) are all Four Number bets. In this example, if 5 were the result on the next spin you would be paid twice at the eight to one rate because 5 is covered in two different bets. There are 22 ways to make this wager.

Five Number Bets

Figure 7

00	3	6	9	12	15	18	21	24	27	30	33	36
	2	5	8	11	14	17	20	23	26	29	32	35
0	1	4	7	10	13	16	19	22	25	28	31	34

There is only *one* Five Number Bet. It is indicated in Figure 7 and can be made by placing your wager in *either* of the positions depicted. As you saw in Figure 2, this is the worst possible wager for the player. The bet covers 0,1,2,3, and 00.

Six Number Bets

Figure 8

00	3	6	9	12	15	18	21	24	27	30	33	36
	2	5	8	11	14	17	20	23	26	29	32	35
0	1	4	7	10	13	16	19	22	25	28	31	34

There are eleven of these bets, three of which are shown in Figure 8. The first chip covers 1,2,3,4,5 and 6. The second chip covers 10,11,12,13,14 and 15. The third covers 19,20,21,22,23 and 24.

OUTSIDE BETS

Figure 9

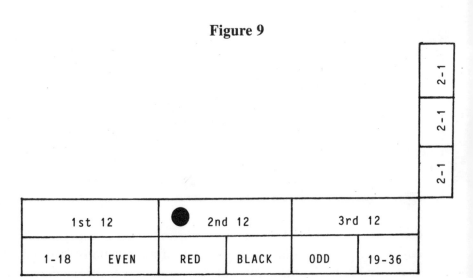

These bets can only be made in the portion of the betting layout shown in Figure 9.

Some of these wagers are paid off at two to one, the rest at even money, but you can only wager the table maximum on those which pay even money.

Dozens

There are only three ways to make this bet. Figure 9 shows a bet covering the dozen numbers from 13-24. Should any of those numbers come up on the next spin, you're a winner.

1-18 or 19-36

Figure 10

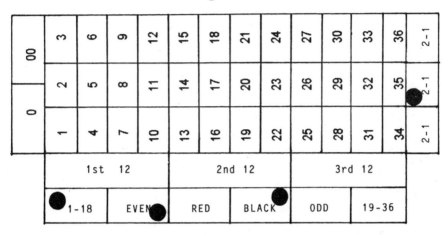

Some people think that since there are only two ways to make this bet, and since the payoff is even money, the player cannot possibly lose. They think that the player, at worst, should break even, winning one and losing the other. Unfortunately, those people forget that whenever the outcome is 0 or 00, they lose both bets. Figure 10 shows a bet on 1-18. The chips do not have to be placed exactly as shown, so long as they are within the boundaries of the 1-18 bet.

Odd or Even

Here you have two choices, both of which pay even money. As long as the outcome of the next spin is an even number, your bet in Figure 10 would win. If the next outcome is an odd number or 0 or 00, you would lose.

Red or Black

As with Even or Odd, 1-18 or 19-36, there are eighteen outcomes that can win this bet for you, twenty that can lose. That's why the pay-off is only even money. In Figure 10 we are going for Black, because that's the way you like your coffee. Does it get anymore scientific than that?

Column Bets

Three choices, all of which pay two to one. Your bet in Figure 10 would win if any of the numbers in that column (2, 5,8,11,14,17,20,23,26,29,32 or 35) come up on the next spin. Twelve numbers can win for you, the other twenty-six lose.

Of course, all these betting options can be mixed in any combination you desire. It's not uncommon to see people making one Two-number bet, a Four-Number bet, a Column bet, and a Dozens bet all at the same time. But don't get carried away in the excitement of the moment. Sometimes people make so many different bets that they end up betting against themselves, putting themselves in a situation where, even if one of their numbers comes up, they can't possibly win enough to cover all the bets that lost.

To my mind, this game is for fun only. There are many systems on the market for winning at Roulette and I've tried most of them with varying degrees of failure. If you play Roulette you will see countless players with pads and pencils tracking the ebb and flow of each number in an attempt to outguess the ball and wheel. But the only way to win at this game is through out-and-out blind luck. If you are lucky enough to win, leave the table with your winnings. If you stay at the table, the generous advantage you give to the casino will soon grind you down.

Note: When betting on Even-Odd, Red-Black, or 1-18 and 19-36 in Atlantic City, the player has an additional option which is very favorable. This option is known as the *en prison* rule. If the player makes one of the even money bets listed above and 0 or 00 is the next outcome, the player has two choices.

1) The player can "imprison" the bet. This means the bet stays where it is. Then, if the bet wins on the next spin, the bet is returned to the player.
2) The player may surrender half of the bet.

The *en prison* option lowers the casino advantage to 2.7% on these bets, making these bets the best on the layout.

Basically, with the *en prison* option, you're given a second chance; you're given new life. Consequently, most people never surrender half their bet, preferring to exercise the *en prison* option. Don't be surprised if the croupier assumes that you will take the *en prison* option. Simply tell him you would prefer to surrender half your bet, if that is what you desire.

If you choose to imprison your bet, the croupier will then mark your chips with a small plastic disc to differentiate them from the other bets on the layout. Then, the very next spin of the wheel will dictate whether that bet is returned to you or whether the casino collects it.

At least one casino in Atlantic City is using a Roulette wheel which contains only 0. 00 is not on the layout. This difference means that the casino's advantage on Inside Bets is reduced from 5.26% to approximately 2.3%. Obviously, if you want to play Roulette you should seek out these tables.

Chapter 5

American Poker

If you have absolutely no knowledge of how to play Poker, please purchase a book which will teach you the basics. It is not my intent in this chapter to help make you a great Poker player, or even a better Poker player. The purpose of this chapter is to explain the differences between how Poker is played in casinos versus how it is played in the normal, friendly (all right, sometimes maybe not so friendly) game you are accustomed to playing in New York, or Nebraska, or wherever you happen to live.

The best reason for playing Poker in a casino is that unlike the other casino games, you are not competing against the house. You are now testing your skill and luck against other people just like yourself. No one has you at a fixed percentage disadvantage.

Yet, even though my reason as stated above is true, I firmly believe that the real reason people enjoy Casino Style Poker is that it gives them a chance to test their skill against some of the best Poker players in the world. You are not playing against your Uncle Fred, who couldn't care less if he loses, or your Aunt Mildred, who still can't remember that she should not fold when all her cards are of the same suit, or your friend Jerry who can be bluffed consistently by anyone who raises more than a quarter. You will now be playing with people who, for the most part, really know how to play. Granted, I've seen players who couldn't pass muster in a penny ante game, let alone a Vegas casino, but these folks are the exception and not the rule. Whether you decide to play in a $1-3 game, or a "no limit" game, the vast majority of the players at your table will be better than the people you play against at home.

For years, I avoided playing Poker at the casinos because I had heard from a number of people that I would be fleeced immediately by the locals regardless of my level of skill. The local players, the story went, had played with each other for years, had developed secret signs to tell each other what they were holding, and would gang up on all the "tourists". Were this true, a person could be trounced severely regardless of skill level. However, once I decided to play, I found that these stories were unfounded. Granted, you may sit in at a game somewhere and encounter a few sharpies playing as a team, but that would definitely be the exception and not the rule. It is true, nonetheless, that I have sat in on a number of games where virtually all of the other players seemed to know each other. This does place the new player at a disadvantage, because the regulars need only figure out one style of play . . . yours. You, on the other hand, need to figure out the style of every other person at the table.

On the low end, most Poker games will fall into the $1- $3 category. On the high end, the sky is the limit. Obviously, you should only play in games you can tolerate financially. No matter how good you think you are, I wouldn't suggest that you tackle the top seven finishers in last years' World Series of Poker until you've tested your skill at a lower level.

Here are the major differences between the Poker you play at home, and the way it's done in the casinos.

TYPES OF GAMES PLAYED

That's right, you will not find any "wild card" games being dealt in the casinos. The fare is basic. Seven Card Stud [both high, low, and high-low split], Texas Hold'em [high only], Omaha [high, and high-low split], and Five Card Draw. If you don't know how to play Seven Card Stud or Five Card Draw, buy a book about Poker. Texas Hold'em, commonly known as Hold'em, is probably the most popular game as I write this.

Due to the fact that so few cards are dealt, Hold'em is a game which accommodates a large number of players. Each player receives two cards down, you bet, there is a "flop" of three cards in the center of the table. These three cards are played as though they were actually in your hand. Of course, they can be used by everyone else, too You bet, there is another flop of one card, you bet, there is a final flop of one card, you bet, and someone wins. If you stay for all the cards, you'll have two in your hand, and five "common" flop cards out in the middle of the table. You must use the two cards in your hand and three of the cards from the flop to make up your five-card hand.

Omaha is similar to Hold'em. Everyone receives four cards down instead of two. The flop is the same; three, one, and one. You bet between all the intervals. This is usually a high-low split game. And even though you have four cards in your possession, and a total of nine cards when the "common" cards are included, you can only play five at a time. In addition, you can only play two from your hand. That's right, you *must* play two from your hand and three from the common cards laying out there in the center of the table. Yes, you can play two of your four cards for low and the other two for high, or you can play the same two, or any combination of the four cards taken two at a time, but you must play two from your hand. And another thing: there is usually no split unless someone has at least an Eight or lower for the low hand. That's correct, if no one has at least an Eight for low the entire pot goes to the high Poker hand. Yes, this makes for a very interesting game.

NUMBER OF PLAYERS

It is not at all uncommon for a table to seat eight to ten players. Yes, I know that you can't play Seven Card Stud with eight players because 7 x 8= 56. However, it's done in the casinos all the time. The reason? There is seldom a hand when all 52 cards are used. Invariably, at least two or three players drop after seeing their first few cards. In the case of Hold'em and Omaha, ten players is more the rule than exception. With Hold'em, the size of the table is the only reason not to have thirteen or sixteen, or, for that matter, twenty-two players. If the table was made that large, however, the players at each end would need opera glasses to see the cards at the other end of the felt.

THE DEALER

When you're playing with your friends, relatives or whomever, you each take turns shuffling and dealing the cards. In the casino game, the casino provides a person to do that for you. Yes, this prevents some card shark from stacking a deck, and is intended to keep the game honest and above board. Dealers typically rotate every twenty or thirty minutes. In addition to dealing the cards, they provide chips when you need to purchase them, watch the pot to make sure all the players are contributing as they should, and announce the winning hands. The dealer is also there to answer any questions you may have, to explain all the basic rules, and settle any minor disputes. Do not hesitate to question the dealers, regardless of how busy they appear to be. It would be very ignorant to play in a game if you're not clear on the rules. For his or her services, the dealer is compensated by the casino and the tips donated by the players. In games where the pot is small, the tip should be at least a quarter or half-dollar. When you win a good size pot, tip a dollar or more. Or, don't tip at all if you don't like the dealer. It's up to you. I think it is interesting to note that the dealers I've interviewed indicate they usually make better tips in the small and medium size games. One told me the story of the hand he dealt which ended with a pot of over $30,000. His tip: nothing.

FIXED BETTING PROCEDURES

At home, if you're playing a game in which the high hand wins, the first bettor will usually be the person with the highest card showing. In the casino, the first bettor will normally be the person with the *lowest* card showing. For games in which there is no card showing, like Hold'em, the first bettor is the person who is seated left of the "button". Never heard of a button? It's simply a small disc which rotates around the table, moving one player at a time after each game, so that the initial bettor is different every game. Another way to think of it is that the button identifies the "pretend" dealer. Since the deal does not rotate, the button does.

The first bet is always a fixed wager, whether it is a quarter, a dollar, or several dollars. Of course this depends on the level of the game you are playing. This first bet is known as the "blind" or "forced" bet, because the person on the hot seat [the first bettor] *must* make this wager. This person does not have the option of folding should he or she not appreciate the first cards dealt to them. The blind bet is always for a fixed amount, say $1 in a $1-$4 game. No more, no less. In some games, there are two blinds or forced bets. The first bettor must make, say, a $1 wager, the next person must make, say, a $2 wager; again, no more, no less. And, finally, there is another type of blind which is called a "live" blind. This describes a situation where everyone who stays in the game calls the bet of the blind, but no one raises. Should this happen, the blind then has the opportunity to raise herself.

After the blind or forced betting has taken place, the rest of the betting must also follow a pattern. In a $1-$3 game of Stud, for example, you may not be able to bet $3 until the last round of cards has been dealt.

If you see a game advertised as $1-$3-$6, this would mean that a wager of $6 is allowed on the final betting round.

There is an ante in some games, none in others. When there is an ante, it is usually fairly small, like a quarter in a $1-$3 game.

Raise, raise, raise. That's correct, in most games the number of raises is limited to three. But, unlike most home games, when there are only two players remaining in the pot, there is no limit to the number of raises allowed. If two of you decide you have a hand that simply cannot lose, then you can raise each other until there is no money left.

Wanna get down and dirty in a completely legitimate manner? Then check and raise. Though this is very uncommon in most home games, it's allowed in virtually every casino Poker room I've ever seen Remember, you're playing with the "big" boys now.

HOUSE TAKE

Did you think the casino was providing this Poker room just so the dealers could make money? The casino needs to collect its share. In Poker rooms, their take is called the "rake". I suppose it got the name from the manner in which the dealers rake the chips into the secured box attached to the table.

The size of the rake varies from game to game Here are some typical examples.

Betting Limit	% of Rake	W/Maximum of
$1 - $3	10	$3.00
$3 - $6	5	$2.50
$1-$2-$4	10	$3.50
$1-$4-$8	5	$2.00

The rake will generally be more in Stud, less in Hold'em. This is because less hands are dealt per hour in Stud, and Hold'em typically has higher pots, so the casino collects the maximum more often. The amount of the rake, plus a list of the games and some of the basic rules is always listed near the entrance to any Poker room. Look until you find it.

MINIMUM BUY-IN

You can't sit down to play unless you have at least X number of dollars in chips. The amount of the buy-in is listed on the same board that tells you the rake, etc. In a typical $1-$3 game, the buy-in would be at least $20.

Once the game has begun, the table stakes rule applies; if you run out of chips you can only play for that portion of the pot to which you contributed. However, most places will allow you to purchase additional chips providing that your money is already on the table. In other words, you buy-in for $20. You place your $20 worth of chips on top of another $30 in cash. The cash counts as chips being on the table, so you can buy more chips at any time during a game.

If you don't already have cash on the table, you cannot go into your pocket, billfold or purse during a game. Of course, you can always purchase more chips between games.

BURN CARDS

This is another way of keeping the game honest. It is possible for players to mark the cards as the game is being played. If a player does this, then they could identify the top card on the deck. To prevent this, the dealer shuffles, someone cuts, and then the dealer burns a card both prior to the beginning of the first round, and before beginning each subsequent round.

PLACING OF CHIPS IN THE POT

At home, when you call a bet, or raise, you toss your chips into the middle of the pile accumulating in the middle of the table. In the Poker Room at the casino, you do it a little differently. Instead of tossing the chips, you *slide* the chips. Instead of sending the chips to the middle of the table, you slide them out slightly in front of your playing position. Instead of sliding your chips out in a stack, you slide them out so that they are slightly spread apart. When you raise, you slide out two rows of bets; one to call, the other to raise. Do it this way, and you'll make life much easier for the dealer and your fellow players. If the chips of each player are distributed as I indicate, a simply glance around the table will tell you who is staying, raising, reraising, etc. After the betting is finished for each round, the dealer then scrapes all the chips into one big pile in the middle of the table.

If you keep heaving your chips into the pile, people like me might very well wonder if you really tossed six chips and not five. Get my drift?

Should you desire to fold, toss your cards into the middle of the table. Yes, now it's okay to toss.

CARDS PLAY

There is no need for you to declare the value or ranking of your hand. The dealer will read your cards and determine whether you have a winning hand. You should know the ranking of your hand, so that you recognize if the dealer makes an error, but the cards play themselves; turn them over and hope you have the best hand.

CONSERVATIVE PLAY

If you're like me, and you're playing at home, and the game is of the nickel-dime-quarter variety, you never drop out of a hand which has even the most remote of possibilities. Consequently, it is not unusual to have seven players contending for a pot after the last round of betting. Obviously, this is something you will rarely, if ever, see in a casino Poker Room. In a Stud game consisting of eight players, the final round will normally see no more than two to four players.

You must decide for yourself how to play your cards. But if you play every hand which contains only marginal possibilities, you will be swallowed alive. If, on the other hand, you are accustomed to playing only those hands which offer sound possibilities, you will fit right in.

SPEED OF PLAY

This is the first thing I noticed when I began playing Casino Style Poker. The game moves much faster than any I had experienced previously. There is not much idle chitchat between players. The dealer makes every attempt to keep the game moving along. The players, overall, are smarter, and take less time to make decisions. I don't mean to imply that any particular game is all business. There is conversation among the players and the dealers. There is joking and wise comments. But the pace is quicker.

Those are the differences which you need to be aware of before you try a Poker Room. The actual playing of the hands still depends on the style, intelligence and experience of the individual player. You can play Stud for hours and never see a winning hand better than 3 of a Kind, then lose with a Straight Flush. You can stay in a game of Hold'em hoping to fill a Flush and accidentally win with a Queen high because everyone else folds. You can stay in a game of Omaha simply because no one else is betting like they have anything, and either get massacred or win with a small pair. It's still Poker. You're playing in a different environment, but it's still Poker.

And always remember this: Real men play real Poker. Well, just kidding. Kinda. Real women play real Poker, too.

Chapter 6

Pai Gow
Poker

Picture this: You've just arrived at a casino you've never before visited. You notice a small group of people clustered around a table in one of the Blackjack pits. You approach the group to see why everyone in the crowd seems to be studying the action taking place on the table. The players at the table consist of five Orientals and one Caucasian. Instead of cards, you see these plastic things on the table which resemble dominoes. No one in the crowd seems to have the slightest understanding of what is happening. The five Orientals at the table seem to be having fun, but the lone Caucasian appears to be slightly perplexed. You look up and notice a sign which announces that the game you are watching is called "Pai Gow".

Okay, now that you have the picture, remember this: Do not even attempt to play this game! Those plastic things that look like dominoes are actually the equivalent of Chinese playing cards. The figures which make them appear to be dominoes are actually Chinese numbers. So, unless you can read Chinese numbers, it is virtually impossible for you to play this game. This is why the five Orientals at the table seem to be having fun, but the lone Caucasian is lost, and no one watching the game can figure out what is happening. Could you play Blackjack if the playing cards contained no numbers or figures? Of course not. So why try to play a game in which you are literally blind?

All of the above is the bad news. Here is the good news. Same scenario: You are walking through a new casino and you see people clustered around a Blackjack table. At the table are seated two Orientals and four players who are not Oriental. There are playing cards distributed in front of each player, but it is obvious the game is not Blackjack. The dealer appears to be performing some sort of ceremony with a canister of dice. You say to yourself: Oh, oh, this must be another one of those crazy games which can only be played by people with mysterious and special knowledge. Well, my friend, you are wrong, wrong, wrong!

The game you are now observing is call Pai Gow <u>Poker</u>. Please note that the first game I talked about was call Pai Gow, and this game is called Pai Gow <u>Poker</u>. Again, unless you can read Chinese numbers, do not even think about playing Pai Gow. But please make every attempt during your next visit to play Pai Gow Poker, because it is an easy game to learn and a fun game to play, particularly if you find the pace of the normal games likeBlackjack and Craps to be too hectic.

Pai Gow Poker is a game which combines elements of the ancient Chinese game of Pai Gow, and the American game of Poker. So, if you have ever played Poker at any level, including Video Poker, you should be able to play Pai Gow Poker. So long as you have a basic understanding of the ranking of winning hands in Poker, you can play this game.

Let's assume you decide to sit in for a few games. Here's what happens: First, you must make a wager. At most tables, the minimum is $10, though you may find more expensive stakes if you're visiting over a weekend. You may think the $10 minimum seems a tad steep for your taste, but don't worry; in the time it takes to play one hand of Pai Gow Poker, you could have played 5-7 hands of Blackjack. As I stated earlier, this game has a nice pace to it, and is not played with the frenzy of some of the other games. As is the case with Blackjack, there will be a small circular or rectangular area on the felt in which you should place the chips for your wager. In fact, all you need to know regarding the table layout is shown in Figure 1.

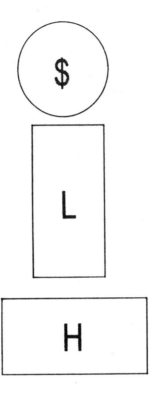

Figure 1

The dealer shuffles the cards and deals seven hands consisting of seven cards each in piles directly in front of her. The players don't get the cards yet. (Once again I am assuming the dealer is female.) She starts dealing from her left, makes seven piles working to her right, then reverses her action, moving from right to left for the second card in the pile, then left to right again, etc. until each pile has exactly seven cards. She then counts the cards remaining in her hand to ensure that she has the correct number of cards remaining. You quickly multiple in your head that seven piles of seven cards each should be a total of 49 cards dealt, which means that she should have 3 cards left out of a single deck of 52 cards, but you are wrong. This playing deck consists of the 52 regular cards, plus one Joker, so when the dealer counts the cards remaining in her hand, she should find four.

The next step is that the dealer picks up a small cup, usually metal, and shakes it to mix up the three dice contained inside. She then flips the cup over, reveals the dice, and counts the total of them. The dice, by the way, look like the same dice used at Craps, except that they are smaller, and each contains the numbers 1 to 6, so that the total of the three dice could be any number from 3 to 18. The total of the dice is what determines which player is to receive the first hand. For, you see, if the piles of cards were distributed in the same order on every hand, the dealer may at times be accused of stacking the deck in her favor. But since the dice determine which hand she will be playing, there is no way for her to predetermine which hand to stack.

The dealer's position is counted as number 1, number 8, or number 15, depending on the total of dice. That is, the <u>Banker's</u> position is counted as number 1, 8, or 15, but since the dealer is almost always the Banker, just think of it that way, and I'll explain the difference later.

Let's assume that the total of the dice was 4. The dealer counts herself as one, the first person to her right as two, the second person as three, and the third person as four. So the third person from her right is given the first hand, which is the first stack on her right, and then the rest of the piles are passed out to player number five, number six, number seven, the dealer, then players number two and three. If this sounds a little confusing, don't worry about it. You have no control over the distribution of the hands. The important issue at this point is that all that stuff, that ritual which looked so mysterious when you were watching other people play this game, is not so mysterious, after all. Also, here is diagram that may help you understand.

Player

7	6	5	4	3	2
14	13	12	11	10	9
—	—	—	18	17	16

Dealer

1

8

15

Keeping this chart in mind, you can see that if the total number from the dice were 4, then the player at the number 4 position would receive the first hand, and the player at position number 3 would receive the last hand.If the total dice number came to 13, then the player at position number 13 (which is also position number 6) would receive the first hand, and the player at position number 12 would receive the last hand. The only time the dealer would receive the last hand would be if the dice total 2, 9, or 16. I hope this makes sense to you, but if it doesn't this will not effect your ability to play the game.

Now you have seven cards in front of you, placed there in a nice, neat stack by the dealer. Your next step is to pick them up, look at them, and hope you can make some sort of Poker hand out of them, Not just one Poker hand, but two. You are going to make up what you can think of as your highest Poker hand, and your second highest Poker hand. All of the other players at the table, plus the dealer, are going to do the same. The object of the game is for your first highest Poker hand to be higher than the dealer's first highest hand, and also for your second highest hand to be higher than the dealer's second highest hand. Some people find it more convenient to think of these two hands as a high hand and a low hand, but since we don't really want a low hand I like to think of it as my best hand and my second best hand.

The ranking of hands is basically the same as in regular Poker; Five Aces, Royal Flush, Straight Flush, Four of a Kind, Full House, Flush, Straight, Three of a Kind, Two Pair, One Pair, and High Card. Those of you who play Poker regularly may now be saying, wait a minute, you can't have a hand of Five Aces unless you have a wild card. And while we are not playing with any truly "wild" cards, you may recall that we are playing with one Joker in the deck. The Joker is an Ace by itself, or it can be used like a "wild" card in Straights, and Flushes. In other words, if you have an Ace and a Joker, you really have two Aces. If you have three Aces and a Joker, you really have four Aces. Should you have an Eight, Nine, Ten, Jack, and Joker, you have a Straight. A hand consisting of Seven, Eight, Ten, Jack, and Joker, would also be a Straight. If you had four spades and the Joker, you have a Flush. If you have a pair of Queens and a pair of Kings, plus a Joker, you really have a pair of Queens, a pair of Kings, and an Ace.

Again, we are going to make two hands out of the seven cards you are now holding. Our best hand will consist of five cards and our second best hand will only consist of two cards. Since most Poker hands consist of five cards, this should not be difficult for us. We simply look at the seven cards, and separate the five which make the best poker hand. This then leaves us with two cards which we can utilize as our second best hand. The ranking of the two-card hand is slightly different merely because it only contains two cards; subsequently the two-card hand cannot contain a Straight, a Flush, or any other ranking except for High Card or a Pair. Sounds easy enough, right? Well, it is a little more complicated than that because you must keep in mind that we want to beat *both* the dealer's best and second best hands. In fact, the only time we win is when we beat *both* of the dealer's hands. What? You mean I gotta beat both of them? Yes, that's what I'm saying, and I know that sounds pretty tough, but the news gets better. On those occasions when we only beat *one* of the dealer's hands, we lose nothing, we gain nothing; we have a draw and no money exchanges hands. And in order for the dealer to collect *our* money, the dealer must either beat or tie both of our hands. Yes, the dealer wins ties. But don't concern yourself too much with the news that the dealer wins ties, because ties seldom occur.

The bottom line here, as they say in the business world, is that you can play a lot of hands without either gaining or losing a lot of money and have a very good time while doing it. This is because if you play your cards properly you won't find many instances of the dealer beating you senseless unless your luck is simply very bad. And the reason for this is that unless we have cards which will make us two good hands, we always play for the tie. Yes, I know this sounds defensive, but it is also intelligent.

Now, one last piece of information you must have in order to play this game. Your best hand, the one which is made up of five cards, *must* be higher than your second best hand. This only makes sense, but this is also where a lot of people end up making mistakes. Should you make the error of arranging your cards so that your second best hand is higher in ranking than your best hand, you lose automatically. You also lose automatically if you mistakenly place only three or four cards in your highest hand, or make any arrangement that does not consist of five cards and two cards.

Let's see if we can make sense out of all of this. You sit down, make a bet of ten dollars, the dealer shuffles, the dealer makes seven little piles in front of her consisting of seven cards each, the dealer shakes the dice, the total of the dice is 9, so the player all the way over at the end of the table (third base in Blackjack lingo) receives the first hand, and the player at position number 15, which is the dealer, gets the last pile of cards.

Your hand consists of the following: Ace of spades(A/S), Queen of spades(Q/S), Joker(J), Nine of diamonds(9/D), Ten of diamonds(10D), Queen of clubs(Q/C), and King of spades(K/S). Get out a deck of cards and deal yourself this exact hand and you'll find this example easier to follow. As you can quickly see, this hand definitely has possibilities. Some people, upon receiving these cards, might immediately arrange their two hands like this:

Highest hand: A/S, J, Q/S, Q/C, K/S

Second highest: 9/D, 10D

This means that their best hand is a pair of Aces (remember the Joker is another Ace), a pair of Queens, and the leftover King. The second best hand is simply the other two leftover cards which did not help the high hand; the Nine and Ten of diamonds. Two pair is not a bad hand, and if you consider the ranking of hands, the dealer would have to have three of a kind or better to beat our two pair for the best hand. So let's assume for a moment that two pair could very well beat the dealer's best hand. Now let's think about the chances we left for our second best hand. Remember, just because it is the second best does not mean that we can merely throw all of our "junk" into this hand and hope for the best. You must think in terms of making the two best hands possible. Bearing this in mind, how else could we play this same hand and improve our chances of winning: A) at least one of the hands, or B) both hands? Well, how about if we made this change:

Highest hand: A/S, J, Q/S, Q/C, 9/D

Second highest: K/S, 10D

Please note that we made just one small change, exchanging the King of spades for the 9 of diamonds. This trade does not effect the ranking of our highest hand, yet makes a definite improvement in our second highest. Or we could alter our thinking entirely, and play the hand this way:

Highest hand: A/S, J, 9/D, 10/D, K/S

Second highest: Q/S, Q/C

Now we are playing a pair of Aces plus trash for the high hand, and a pair of Queens for the second highest. The thinking here is that while our pair of Aces may not win for high, our pair of Queens will almost assuredly win for the second highest and we will come out of this with no worse than a tie.

And now for those of you who thought I had overlooked one of our best possibilities, what if we remembered that our Joker can be used as the fifth card if we have four towards a Straight or Flush, and thus arrange our cards like this:

Highest hand: 9/D, 10/D, J, Q/C, K/S

Second highest: A/S, Q/S

A Straight for the best hand is quite powerful, almost a certainty to beat the dealer's high hand, and the Ace and Queen we have leftover for the second best hand is also very playable. Arranging the cards in this manner provides us with nearly a "lock" for best, and a good shot at also winning second best.

Always remember that we want to arrange our cards so that we have a chance of winning at least one of the hands. I am sure that some readers will take the "macho" approach, think that playing for a tie is like kissing their sister, and put all their high cards in the best hand. The rest of us, however, will play more conservatively, keep more of our money, and play longer on less money even when we don't get decent cards.

Another example: You are dealt the Deuce of clubs(2/C), the Four of hearts(4/H), the Six of hearts(6/H), the Seven of diamonds(7/D), the

Seven of hearts(7/H), the Eight of diamonds(8/D), and the Nine of clubs(9/C). How do you arrange your hand? What about this:

Highest hand: 2/C, 4/H, 6/H, 8/D, 9/C

Second highest: 7/D, 7/H

Obviously, the person who would arrange their hand in this manner is thinking that the trash is worthless, so why not put it in the high hand and save the pair of Sevens for the second best hand. The logic sounds okay at first, but the result is that this person will lose their bet. Why? Because their second best hand carries a higher ranking than their best hand, which is definitely against the rules. This person has no choice but to arrange this hand thusly:

Highest hand: 7/D, 7/H, 2/C, 4/H, 6/H

Second highest: 8/D, 9/C

Yes, I know that this hand appears to have no chance of winning, but strange things happen. Every once in a while, the dealer is dealt a hand that contains Cow Pie. Cow Pie is just the opposite of Pai Gow, and kind of rhymes, so some player some time in history decided the term Cow Pie was appropriate for describing a dealer hand which contains absolutely nothing; a hand even worse than the hand I described immediately before this paragraph. So even when you receive terrible cards, do not despair. As with other games of chance, you can sometimes win with terrible cards and lose with fantastic cards.

Let's consider one more hand and contemplate our options. You receive the Ace of spades(A/S), the Nine of spades(9/S), the Jack of spades(J/S), the Ten of diamonds(10/D), the Joker(J), the Seven of spades(7/S), and the Three of spades(3/S). You immediately recognize that you have a very nice spade Flush and arrange your hands like this:

Highest hand: J/S, 9/S, 7/S, 3/S, J

Second highest: A/S, 10/D

Good job. That is precisely how this hand should be played. But did you also notice that this hand contains a Straight, and could be arranged like this:

Highest hand: J/S, 10/D, 9/S, J, 7/S

Second highest: A/S, 3/S

However, why would anyone in their right mind want to play a Straight for high with an Ace, Three for second best, when they could have a Flush for high with an Ace, 10 for second?

Hopefully, these examples have shown some of the choices you'll need to make in order to play this game. You will not be rushed for time, so think twice about your selections.

For now, let's assume your hand was the one we just finished talking about, with the spade Flush for high and the Ace, 10 for second best. Here's what happens next: First you place the best (five-card hand) in a little rectangular box drawn on the table felt which is usually vertical and labeled with an "H". The second best (two-card hand) goes into another box outlined on the table, normally labeled "L" as in low and located immediately above the box for the highest hand. As stated earlier, the casino thinks of this as a high hand and a low hand, but I like to think of it as the highest hand and the second highest hand.

You weren't supposed to look at the cards of the other players when they picked them up, but I always try to get a glimpse if possible. The casino doesn't want any players combining cards for better hands, or discussing their individual cards, but don't worry too much about this aspect of the game unless someone infers that you should not try to stretch the rules.

Once all the players have their hands aligned in the boxes on the table, the dealer reveals all seven of the cards dealt to her. That's right, up to now she has been waiting for the players to do their thing, and now it's her turn. She turns over her cards, and you hope to see Cow Pie, but this time you are disappointed. Let's assume the dealer has a hand like this: Ten of hearts, Ten of clubs, Five of clubs, Five of diamonds, Jack of spades, Seven of diamonds, and Three of hearts. There is no doubt about what the dealer is going to do with this hand. It will be played like this:

Highest hand: 10/H, 10/C, J/S, 7/D, 3/H

Second highest: 5/C, 5/D

The reason the dealer plays in this manner is logical if you think about it. The dealer is playing for the tie, hoping that while she will probably lose with only one pair in her high hand, she will win most of the second best hands with a low pair. The dealer is playing not to lose. Remember that you are only playing against the dealer, but the dealer is playing against the entire table. She could arrange her hand so that it contained the two pair for the best hand and the Jack, 7 for second best, but then she would lose to everyone at the table who had three of a kind or better for best hand, and a Queen or better for second best.

The next step is that the dealer exposes the hands of the players, starting at third base and working backwards (counterclockwise) around to first base. All hands are compared to the dealer's hands, cards and bets for hands that are losers are collected as she works her way around the table, ties and winners are left out until she is done, then settled as required.

And then another hand begins.

Now, does that sound all that difficult? Of course not.

The game moves at a nice pace, you're not at all rushed, you do not win or lose on every hand because of the ties which occur, and there is probably not a pit boss standing over your shoulder. So, as I concluded after learning how to play this game, everyone should play. But, I should mention some other details before we finish up on this topic.

First, when you lose your bet, it is gone. However, when you win a bet, a 5% commission is collected, which is something similar to Baccarat. However, unlike Baccarat, this 5% charge on winning wagers is normally collected immediately at the end of each hand.

Even though you actually only win $9.50 for every $10.00 bet, I still think Pai Gow Poker is a worthy game. As you can figure for yourself, your disadvantage is at least the 5% commission you pay only on winning wagers, plus the fact the dealer wins all ties. And while a 5%+ disadvantage means you have better odds at other games, Pai Gow Poker is every bit as fun as Roulette or Video Poker, and can provide a rest from the frenzy of Blackjack or Craps without creating exposure to truly ridiculous odds like those associated with Keno or Slot Machines.

Banker. Remember when I mentioned the Banker early on in this chapter? I said that since the dealer is ordinarily the Banker, I would leave this for the end. Well, this is the end, so here's what you need to know about the Banker.

First, you, yes you, can be the Banker should you desire. Simply let the dealer know that you want to be the Banker and she will be sure to accommodate you. Being the Banker means that you are the person who either collects from or pays off all of the players at the table depending upon whether your hand is better or worse than theirs. In other words, you replace the dealer and everyone is playing against you.

However, being the Banker does not relieve you of the problem of beating the dealer. When a player is also the Banker, the first thing that happens is that the dealer compares her hand with the Banker's hand. She wins, loses, or ties, just like the players. The dealer then exposes all the rest of the hands, determines whether they win or lose when compared to the Banker's hand, then assists the Banker in either collecting or paying off bets. Yes, the house still collects the 5% commission on winning wagers.

Other than wanting to seem important, there is a legitimate reason for being the Banker. The Banker wins all ties. So if the player loses one hand(5-card) and ties the other(2-card), he or she lose their wager.

I have never been the Banker, even though winning all ties does improve the odds against me, for the simple reason that I play this game to relax between serious gambling sessions at Craps or Blackjack. Why would I want to make myself tense by worrying about whether I can beat everyone at the table? Should you choose to be the Banker, I suggest you study the betting habits of the other players at the table. If the other players are wagering more than you can collectively afford to pay off, don't become the Banker.

As stated previously, the key to this game is deciding how to split your cards to: A) give yourself the best chance of winning both hands, or B) come out of it by winning at least one of the hands and thereby gaining a tie. Of course, at times, it will be impossible to accomplish either. So keep this rule of thumb in mind when you try this game: Regardless of the ranking of your 5-card hand, try to play so that your 2-card hand contains at least a King. For example, if you have two pairs plus an additional King, you can consider keeping the two pairs in your

5-card hand. Should you have two pair and no King, then you must place the highest pair in your 5-card hand, and the smaller pair in your 2-card hand. In other words, if you can't keep at least a King in your 2-card hand, play for the tie.

The money management advice supplied earlier for Blackjack should also be applied in this game.

If you haven't yet tried Pai Gow Poker, you've missed an entertaining and stimulating game. So, get with the program and give it a try!

Chapter 7

Caribbean Stud

What a perfect game for the casinos of the world; one that combines elements of 5-card Stud Poker with slot machines. Does it get any better than this? You can actually play a real game of Poker and at the same time try for a giant jackpot like those offered by various banks of progressive slot machines; jackpots which can easily reach over $100,000! Nearly anyone can play because the only tool needed by the player is a rudimentary knowledge of Poker. Yes, anyone who knows the ranking of Poker hands can attack this game. And those who have played 5-card Stud Poker will find this game to be a snap. However, as is the case with most casino games, the casino has a large, virtually unbeatable edge.

Like most of the newer games which have been introduced over the past several years, this one is normally found in the Blackjack pit, and is played on a table which resembles a Blackjack table. The first difference with this game is that you have the opportunity of placing *three* separate wagers. The first is simply your Ante Bet, and at most locations this will range anywhere from $2-3 dollars all the way up to $100, sometimes more. You will find a square at your playing position clearly marked "Ante", so don't worry about where to place this wager.

The second wager is known as the Progressive Jackpot Bet. It is only $1, never more and never less, and automatically qualifies you to participate in the pool for the Progressive Jackpot. Except for the fact that there is no handle for you to pull, making this wager is like playing a slot machine. Yes, it only takes a buck to win a jackpot which could be well over a hundred thousand dollars. There is even an electronic display board at the table, with a meter that continuously rolls up the numbers just like the progressive payoffs at the slot machines. For this wager, there is a Drop Slot at your playing position. Should you desire to make this bet, simply stick a dollar token into the slot prior to the deal.

The third wager, called the Bet To Call The Dealer (hereafter called the BTCTD), is slightly different in that it is not made until *after* you receive your cards. Like the other two betting options, this one is also clearly marked on the table in a square labeled "Bet". Should you decide you have a hand which can beat the dealer's hand, you *must* make a wager which is exactly twice the amount of your Ante Bet. If you don't like your cards, you can fold and thereby surrender your Ante Bet. Sound easy enough? Of course. So let's review what happens when you try this game.

First you purchase chips. Next, you make your Ante Bet. You will note a spot in front of your playing position clearly labeled "Ante". We will assume your Ante Bet is $5. At the same time you make the Ante Bet, prior to the dealing of the cards, you may also place a Progressive Jackpot Bet. Unlike the Ante Bet, this wager is not mandatory. Later on we will get into more detail about the Progressive Jackpot Bet.

Okay, you've anted $5. Each player and the dealer are then dealt five cards. At some casinos, a very human dealer will shuffle the cards and then deal seven stacks of five cards in front of himself. Yes, for those of you who have noticed, I'm finally going to assume the dealer is male. And at some places he will be dealing out of the hand. At others, the shuffling is done by a machine located to the dealers left. It is called a Shuffle Master because it shuffles the cards, and is manufactured by a company called Shuffle Master. The reason the Shuffle Masters have been introduced is so that the casino can create more "action". The Shuffle Master eliminates the time when the dealer would ordinarily be shuffling the cards. Less human shuffling means more actual playing time, which means more money in play. At some tables, the Shuffle Master actually deals out the hands, five cards at a time. At others, the dealer retrieves the shuffled cards from the machines and then deals the hands. Regardless of how the cards are shuffled or dealt, you will end up with a hand of five cards placed face down in front of your position. The dealer's cards are dealt four face down, and the last face up.

At this point you pick up your cards (it is okay to use both hands) and decide whether you have a hand worth playing. The question to be answered here is whether you think you can beat the dealer's hand. Yes, in this regard it is a little like Pai Gow Poker. I say this because a hand containing nothing higher than an Eight may win. Conversely, a Straight may lose. There is a basic strategy which can be used in this game, but we will get to that later.

We will assume that you have picked up your cards and you have a very playable hand; let's say 3 Kings. This is a terrific hand. So good we decide there is almost no chance of the dealer's cards beating us. So, now we exercise the BTCTD option by playing $10 worth of chips in the section of the layout labeled "Bet". This wager *must* be exactly and precisely twice our Ante Bet. Had our Ante Bet been $15, the Bet To Call The Dealer would have to be $30. Had the Ante Bet been $27, the BTCTD would have to be $54.

A quick glance around the table of seven players indicates that five of them are not pleased with their hands. All five of those players fold by placing their cards face down adjacent to the Slot Drop. There is no question about whether they are folding, because none of them placed additional chips in the Bet section.

The other two players plus yourself, who have decided to play out the hand, place their cards face down anywhere near the Ante Bet location. This move, when combined with the action of adding chips to the Bet section, make it clear to the dealer that we plan on taking some of his money.

Now that we have all made our intentions clear, the dealer starts picking up the cards of those players who are going no further in this game. He begins at what we know from Blackjack as third base and works back toward first. As he collects the cards, he places each hand in front of himself and spreads the cards to count them, to ensure each hand contains five cards. The reason he counts the discards? Some players may want to cheat by "saving" cards which they can slip back into the game when those cards can be more useful. Yes, again, the casino has to protect its backside.

Once all the discards have been picked up, the dealer reveals his cards and we find out whether we hand won or lost. However, it is not as easy as our hand simply beating the dealer's hand. Here's why: In order for the dealer to be in a position of contesting the hand, the dealer's cards *must* contain at least an *Ace/King*. If the dealer does not have at least an Ace/King, there is no contest. The dealer basically surrenders. The result is that you win the Ante Bet. That's right, the Ante Bet and only the Ante Bet. Should the dealer's hand not reflect an Ace/King we have no chance of winning the BTCTD.

Now let's consider several possible outcomes for this hand of 3 Kings. (It might be beneficial to take out a deck of cards and actually deal these hands so all is easily understood.)

1) The dealer shows the following: Ace of Diamonds, Queen of Spades, Ten of Clubs, Eight of Hearts, Seven of Clubs. Does the dealer hand qualify? No way. The dealer has an Ace/Queen, which definitely is not higher than Ace/King. Consequently, even though we have a very nice Three of a Kind, we win only our Ante Bet. In this example, that amounts to $5. The other bet we made, the $10 BTCTD, we pull off the table. The dealer pays off our winning Ante Bet and collects our cards. At this point, there is a difference in the standard operating procedure at various casinos. Some do not even bother to look at our cards. The fact of the matter is that we have won the Ante Bet regardless of what our hand contains, so why even bother showing the hand? The answer takes us back to that Progressive Jackpot Bet we might have made. Some casinos automatically reveal our cards just in case we might have a hand that qualifies for a jackpot payoff.

2) Different cards for the dealer: Ace of Spades, King of Diamonds, Queen of Clubs, a Deuce and a Three. Now what happens? Did the dealer qualify? Absolutely! Ace/King/Queen is definitely higher than Ace/King. And now it's time for us to rejoice. For, not only are we paid even money on our Ante Bet, we are paid at the rate of 3:1 on the three lovely Kings. Follow me on this. We had $5 on the Ante Bet, and $10 on the BTCTD. So how much do we win? $5 on the Ante Bet, and $30 on the BTCTD. A nifty net profit of $35. Hooray for our side.

3) Change the scenario again. This time let's give the dealer these cards: Jack of Diamonds, Ten of Spades, Nine of Clubs, Eight of Hearts and Seven of Clubs. Yes, that's a nice little Straight. Yes, a Straight beats the dickens out of our 3 Kings. So we lost not only the $5 Ante Bet, but also the $10 BTCTD. Like any other game, you pay your money and take your chances. There will be times when you will win with a Jack high and lose with a Full House.

These three examples provide nearly everything you need to know in order to play this game. In example #2, we won the hand and received a payoff of 3:1. The casinos call this a Bonus Payout. Though there may be some small differences, Figure 1 displays a typical Bonus Payout Schedule.

Figure 1

BONUS PAYOUT SCHEDULE

1 pair	1:1
2 pairs	2:1
3 of a kind	3:1
Straight	4:1
Flush	5:1
Full House	7:1
4 of a kind	20:1
Straight Flush	50:1
Royal Flush	100:1

One additional comment regarding the payoffs shown in Figure 1. All of the payoffs should contain this addendum: up to table maximum. The reason? Let's assume for a moment you feel you have just received a sign from God. And He instructs you to bet $100 on the next hand of Caribbean Stud. You do so and are dealt a wonderful sight; a Royal Flush. Better yet, the dealer qualifies, so you are about to receive 100 times your $100 wager. Or are you? What is 100 X 100? That's right, it's 10,000. What is the table maximum? Probably no more than $3,000. So do you collect $10,000 for your Royal Flush? Absolutely not. Sorry, Charlie. However, your Royal Flush did win the Progressive Jackpot.

Or did it? Did you drop $1 into the Drop Slot before this hand? If you did, you win the Progressive Jackpot. Congratulations. Not only did you collect from the Bonus Payout, you also won the Jackpot.

Now, you ask, what would I have won had I drawn the Royal Flush at a time when the dealer could not produce a qualifying hand? Good question. As stated earlier, the dealer's hand *must* qualify in order for us to collect our BTCTD, which is paid off at the rates shown in Figure 1. This, however, is not the case when we are talking Progressive Jackpot. Each and every time you place that $1 in the Drop Slot, you qualify for the following payoffs no matter how high or low the hand of the dealer. Does this mean that if we have a Full House and the dealer beats us with a Straight Flush that we still win? Yes, if we are talking about the Progressive Payouts. So we could actually *lose* the BTCTD and still win a payout from the Progressive. And as strange as that may sound, simply keep in mind that the Progressive Payouts and the $1 we nudged into the Drop Slot have nothing whatsoever to do with whether we win or lose our Ante Bet or the BTCTD. Figure 2 shows the standard Progressive Payouts:

Figure 2

HAND	PROGRESSIVE PAYOFF
Flush	$50
Full House	$100
Four-of-a-Kind	$250
Straight Flush	10% of Jackpot
Royal Flush	100% of Jackpot

As was the case with Figure 1, there is a small addendum to these payoffs. Should multiple hands qualify for the Progressive Jackpot during the same hand, the winners share the total Jackpot in ascending order. Here's what this means. We will assume that five of you are playing and that each of you has one of the hands listed in Figure 2. We will also assume that the Jackpot has grown to a nice even $100,000. So here is how the money is spread out. The plain old Flush receives $50. The Full House collects $100. The person with the 4-of-a-Kind is presented $250. Now add those up. $50 + $100 + $250 = $400. We subtract $400 from $100,000, which leaves us with $99,600. The stiff who was lucky enough to draw the Straight Flush receives 10% of that total, which is $9,960. And you, the sharp player who has the Royal Flush? You get everything that is left over. So $99,600 - $9,960 = $89,640. Granted, it's a shame you had to share the Progressive Jackpot, but $89,640 is still a nice payoff.

Is this game easy enough? Of course. Should we play it? Well, let's take a look at the odds against us. This is basically a game of 5-card Stud. And in 5-card Stud, there are a total of 2,598,960 possible hands which could be dealt to us. Figure 3 shows both the type and number of hands which are possible.

Figure 3

ONE DECK
FIVE-CARD POKER HANDS

TYPE OF HAND	TOTAL POSSIBLE
Royal Flush	4
Straight Flush	36
Four of a kind	624
Full House	3,744
Flush	5,108
Straight	10,200
Three of a kind	54,912
Two pair	123,552
One pair	1,098,240
No pair	1,302,540

You can see that the types of hands we are going to draw most frequently are in the no-pair and one-pair categories. Figure 4 now shows, based on the above mathematics, how often we can expect to draw any of the hands shown in Figure 3.

Figure 4

Type of hand	Can expect 1 out of every:
Royal Flush	648,740 hands
Straight Flush	72,193 hands
Four of a kind	4,165 hands
Full House	694 hands
Flush	508 hands
Straight	255 hands
Three of a kind	47 hands
Two pair	21 hands
One pair	2.4 hands
No pair	2.0 hands

Now go back and compare Figure 4 with the payoffs shown in Figures 1 and 2. If we have a winning Full House, according to the Bonus Payout Schedule we will be paid at the rate of 7:1. However, Figure 4 shows that we will only draw a Full House once in every 694 hands. The true payoff should be 694:1. Do we see a casino advantage here?

The odds of us hitting a Royal Flush are 648,740:1. So if we hit one for our $1 Progressive Jackpot Bet, we should receive $648,740. Is that what we collect? Of course not. The largest Jackpot paid to date was slightly over $300,000, and the average probably runs more in the range of $100,000. Do we see a casino advantage here? Of course. And it's huge.

Return again to that Progressive Jackpot. What happens when somebody hits it? Does it start all over again at a base of, say, $50,000? No. At most places it starts over again at a base of $10,000. In addition, about 46% of every dollar that is deposited into the Drop Slot goes to the casino, the rest stays in the pot. Are we stupid enough to make bets where the casino has a 46% casino advantage? Should we, or should we not play this game? Consider the following:

1) Playing for the Progressive Jackpot payoff is very much like playing slot machines or investing in your State's Lottery. In fact, at odds of 648,740 to 1, you have a greater chance of drawing a Royal Flush than of winning the lottery. However, would you travel down to your local store, stand at their counter, and purchase a lottery

ticket every five or six minutes for the next three or four hours? After all, the payoff could be huge, so for $1 it might be worth *your* money. Not *my* money, because I don't play lotteries. In Caribbean Stud the casino is playing on our greed. Everybody wants to hit the huge payday. Just remember that you can play this game without donating to the Progressive Jackpot.

2) In terms of the Bonus Payout Schedule, the casino's advantage is not as severe as it first seems. Keep in mind that you hold the advantage of being able to look at your cards prior to deciding whether to double your basic Ante Bet. Also, the casino pays off every time the dealer does not qualify.

3) Now think about number 2, above. Don't forget that just because you have a wonderful hand doesn't mean you're going to win a Bonus Payout. Remember that the dealer must have a qualifying hand. Consequently, a lot of player Pairs, 3-of-a-Kinds and Straights go unpaid. So maybe the odds *are* as bad as they seem.

The most sound advice I can give you for this game is that you should not consider making a BTCTD unless you have at least a pair. As shown in Figure 4, that should happen approximately every 2.4 hands. As I stated earlier, this is a game where a small pair can win one hand, and then a Straight will get beat the next. I once sat at a table where the dealers went over forty-five minutes without producing a qualifying hand. All of us at the table, once we picked up on what was happening, started making the BTCTD on every hand regardless of what we were holding. When the dealers are that cold, it would be ignorant not to. Needless to say, the entire table enjoyed healthy profits. Yet, I have also sat at a table where over the course of five incredible hands the dealer never had anything less than a Flush.

MONEY MANAGEMENT

Should you decide to try this game, it will require some of your "serious" money. The stakes are too high to try this with "fun" money. The only question is how much money you want to risk. This is not a case of being able to work the odds in your favor, so you must rely basically on luck. If you are drawing terrific hands, you are at the right table. If you are drawing great hands but the dealer can't qualify, or if you're drawing terrible hands, you may be at the wrong table at the wrong time. The trick is to find the right table at the right time. When you do, like all of the other games, keep increasing your basic playing unit when you are winning. Reduce it if you begin to lose.

One additional comment regarding money management. Should you decide to keep popping that $1 into the Drop Slot to qualify for the Progressive Jackpot, you are committing suicide. Yes, I realize that it's a gamble. I know you could win a giant jackpot. I also know the dealer's sometimes will look at you like you're really stupid if you don't drop that $1. But none of that can be overcome by the fact that in terms of the odds against us, this is a horrible bet.

Chapter 8

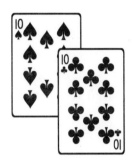

Let It Ride

Here is still yet another of those games which is based on Poker. In order to play, you need only a basic understanding of the ranking of Poker hands. Sound easy? It is. And what is even better, here is finally a game where 1) you are not competing against the dealer, and 2) you actually want the dealer to have a good hand. Yes, as strange as it may sound, in this game it would be wonderful if the dealers could manage to deal themselves a high pair on each and every hand. Like all of the other Poker-based games, this one is also found in the Blackjack pit. The basic idea here is that we will be dealt three cards, and then the dealer will reveal two more cards common to all hands. So we will end up with a total of five cards, just like in 5-card Stud Poker. We will win or lose depending on the strength of our 5-card hand. Figure 1 shows the typical payoffs the casino will provide for us if we can produce, at the minimum, a pair of Tens.

Figure 1

OUR HAND	PAYOFF
Royal Flush	1000-1
Straight Flush	200-1
4 of a Kind	50-1

Full House	11-1
Flush	8-1
Straight	5-1
3 of a Kind	3-1
Two Pair	2-1
Pair of 10's or better	1-1

Figure 2, which follows, tells us everything we need to know regarding the table layout.

Figure 2

To begin this game, you *must* make three wagers. As shown in Figure 2, there are three betting circles; #1, #2, and #$. Minimums required for this game range from $2 and up, so note the requirements when you join the game. For our discussion, we will assume a minimum wager of $5, so it will take $15 for us to play this first hand. Repeating myself, we *must* place one $5 chip in each of the betting circles.

Next, will come the deal. As noted in the chapter on Caribbean Stud, the cards may come from a Shuffle Master, or the dealer may actually shuffle and deal out of the hand. Either way, you are going to receive three cards, all dealt face down. So, pick up your cards. Yes, it's okay to use both hands. No, it is not okay to show your cards to the other players, though some casinos are more strict about this rule than others.

Okay, we have three bets on the table, and three cards in our hand. The dealer has two cards in front of him, both facing down so we can't see them. Now it is time to make the first of two decisions. The question is this: Do our first three cards offer enough possibilities to warrant us remaining in the game? Remember that it takes at least a pair of Tens to collect a payoff. If the answer is yes, we simply slide our three cards under the bet labeled as #1. This is done in the same manner as sliding your cards beneath your chips in Blackjack. If the answer is no, we can have our first bet removed from the board. We do this by scraping our cards against the felt just like we do in Blackjack when we want an additional card. Should this be our decision, the dealer will then nudge our chips off of bet #1 and back toward us. Easy enough?

Once all the players have made this first decision, the dealer picks up one of the two cards in front of his position and turns it face up for all to see. Since this game could also be termed a shortened version of the Poker game known as Hold'em, some people refer to this as the "flop". In some casinos, usually when the cards are dealt by the dealer out of the hand, the two dealer cards are dealt off the deck. However, this is the exception and not the rule. Anyway, we now have the opportunity of seeing the dealer's first card. Right. Now we must make yet another decision, which will be both our second and last. The question now is whether the three cards in our hand, plus the fourth card out there in front of the dealer, when added together, still warrant us staying in the game. Should we still not like our possibilities, we scrape our cards again and the dealer will nudge our chips off the bet marked #2. If our 4-card hand warrants playing, we slide our cards under the bet marked with the $ sign. But, you may wonder, why not slide them under the bet marked #2, since that would seem to be the logically place to slide them? The answer is that once this second decision is made, we have no more decisions to make and the game is now out of our control. For, you see, regardless of our decision at this point we are automatically in the rest of the way. We can toss our cards on top of our chips, adjacent to them, or we can slide them under the bet marked $. Either way, the money in the $ betting circle is going to stay there. We have no choice concerning that wager.

Next, the dealer flops another card in front of his playing position, giving us a total of five cards; three in our hand, plus both the dealer's cards. Did we win? That depends on whether all five cards can generate, at the minimum, a pair of Tens. If they do, we are paid as shown in Figure 1. If they don't, the dealer takes our money.

Let's get specific. As before, deal these practice hands to yourself so you don't become confused.

1) We've got thirty dollars on the table; $10 on each spot. Our three cards are the Ten of Clubs, the Ten of Spades, and the Eight of Spades. What is our decision on the first bet? Are you kidding? This is a No-Brainer. As shown in Figure 1, a pair of Tens pays at even money. We cannot possibly lose! We can only improve this hand. Consequently, we slide all three cards, face down, beneath the bet marked with the $ sign. This way the dealer knows that we are in the game all the way to the end. The dealer also knows that unless we have lost our mind, we probably already have a winning hand. The dealer then flops a Four of Hearts, which is of no help to us. But don't give up yet on improving the hand. Remember, this is one game where we fervently wish the dealer good luck. In this case, the dealer catches another Four on the last card, and all of a sudden we have two pair, which pays 2:1. For each spot on which we still have a bet, we receive $20. Since we still have all three betting spots covered, we collect a total of $60 in profits. Again, anytime we have a winner in the first three cards, we slide the cards under the bet marked with the $ sign.

2) Our three cards are the Four of Spades, the Five of Diamonds, and the Eight of Clubs. What is our decision on bet #1? What do we have? Think about it. At best, we have three cards to a possible Straight. What are our chances of the dealer coming up with a Seven and a Six? Is this a joke? We have almost No chance. So we scrape our cards on the table and the dealer nudges our $10 off the first betting circle. The dealer's first card just happens to be the Six of Hearts. Now the decision becomes a tad more difficult. We must think for all of three seconds. Why only three seconds? Well, what's the chance of us filling an inside Straight? And if we don't fill the Straight, does our four-card hand offer any other winning possibilities? The second answer is that while we could pair up on the fifth card, we still wouldn't have the minimum of a pair of Tens. The answer to the first question is that we have nearly no chance. Yet, for those who enjoy a gamble, we will assume that we have decided to "Let It Ride"! So we slide our cards under either bet #2 or the bet marked $. It makes no difference. Now we have $20 on the table riding on whether the dealer can come up with a Seven. Does he?

Of course not. You're out $20. And if you continue to draw on hands that offer such terrible possibilities, you deserve to lose.

3) With this hand we immediately see a lot of red; the King ofDiamonds, the Ten of Diamonds, and the Ace of Diamonds. What's our first decision? Again, this is a No-Brainer! First of all, we have three cards to a Royal Flush. Second, we have three cards to a plain old Flush. Third of all, we have three cards to a Straight. Fourth of all, we have three cards, any of which would make us a winner if it can be matched. Consequently, we slide our cards under bet #1, which tells the dealer we have some good potential here. The dealer then flops over the Six of Diamonds. Darn it! Several of our possibilities have just been destroyed. No Royal Flush, no Straight. Now we've lost confidence. So, even though we still have the possibility of catching the Flush, we scrape, and the dealer pushes bet #2 back to us. The fifth card? It's the King of Clubs and we're a winner. For having the foresight to stay on bet #1, we collect $20; $10 on bet #1, and $10 on the bet marked with the $. Some might say we should have stayed on all three bets, and I agree. With four cards to a Flush you gotta go for it. Particularly since we also had high cards which could match up. This does, however, raise a philosophical question. Are you playing three bets of $10, or one bet of $30? Answer that question for yourself *before* you begin to play.

4) We receive the Five of Spades, the Five of Hearts, and the Ten of Clubs. First decision? Before you answer, ask yourself this question: Beginning with the three cards I am holding, what is the absolute best 5-card hand I can end up with should the dealer flop the exact cards I want? In this example, the answer is obvious: We could end up with four Fives, but only if the dealer manages to come up with another pair of them. Yet, it's possible. Right? So maybe you're thinking of "Letting It Ride" on bet #1. And then just before you make that decision, the person seated to your right says, "A lousy pair of Fives. Why couldn't they be Tens?" You think she's talking about *your* hand, then realize she's talking about *hers*. So now what is our chance of ending with four Fives? Nonexistent. And, you see, this is why some casinos are quite strict about players

discussing their cards or showing their cards to each other. Anyway, we scrape off bet #1. The dealer's first flop card is a Jack of Spades. We scrape bet #2. The dealer's last card is an Eight of Hearts. We lose the bet marked $. Had the person seated at our right not revealed their hand, we might have stayed in for at least bet #1. Consequently, while we lost, it was only $10 instead of $20 or $30.

Simple enough? Yes, and no. Most hands are very easy to play, but then when you are dealt those Straight and Flush possibilities and "Let It Ride" on all the bets, you can be burned severely. What is our disadvantage in this game? Go back to the Chapter on Caribbean Stud and check out Figure 3, then compare it to Figure 1 from this chapter. For example: The odds of drawing Three of a Kind are approximately 47 to 1. What's the actual payoff from the Payoff Schedule? 3 to 1. Anybody see a casino advantage here? Well, it's not as bad as it sounds. Think of it this way. You give me $30. I give you three cards. If you don't like the first three cards, I will refund $10 of your money. Then I'll give you another card, and if you don't like it, I'll refund another $10. Granted, the payoffs aren't great, but the player definitely has the advantage when it comes to controlling the money.

MONEY MANAGEMENT

As is the case with several of the other games we have discussed, how you manage your money in this game is pretty much dependent on whether you are running hot or cold. If you can't draw at least a pair of Tens over the first three or four hands you play, leave the table. If you can't draw any kind of decent hand, but the dealer keeps dealing himself a pair of Kings, stay right where you are. Can we keep it anymore simple than that? When you're winning, increase your basic unit. When you're losing, reduce your basic unit or abandon the game.

There is a nice pace to this game and it is easy to play, so give it a try.

Chapter 9

Red Dog

Although the casinos call this game Red Dog, most of you have probably already heard of it under names such as Acey-Deucy, In-Between, Between the Sheets, or Split the Sheets. This is a game which may have been played by your great grandfather if he was a cowboy or miner, or a man who frequented the bars of the wild west back in the 1800s. The rules are extremely simple and the game can be fun to play, even though this is another game where the odds are stacked heavily against you.

Red Dog tables are generally found adjacent to, in the middle of, or somewhere close to the Blackjack tables. It is played on a Blackjack table, but the felt reflects a different layout. There is a dealer. There is a shoe containing at least six decks. You begin by placing a wager. The dealer exposes two cards by placing them face up in front of his position. The question is: Will the value of the next card off the deck fall between the value of the two exposed cards? Aces are always high. If there is no spread between the first two cards, like a Nine and a Ten, there is an automatic tie; you neither win nor lose, and a new round begins. If the spread is at least one card, you have a decision to make prior to the dealer exposing the third card. You can leave your wager as it is, or you can double it. That's right, you really only have two decisions in this game. First, you must decide on the size of your initial wager. Second, you must decide whether to double your wager.

On those occasions when the first two cards exposed by the dealer are the same [a pair], you cannot double your bet. [Don't worry, you can't lose if this happens.] The dealer draws a third card to see if Three of a Kind can be made. If Three of a Kind is not made, you have a tie, or push, and a new round begins. Should the third card make Three of a Kind, the players are all paid off at the rate of 11 to 1. This sounds very nice, except that the true payoff for this wager should be 24 to 1. However, why complain when the bet is essentially free?

The payoffs for all bets are dependent upon the spread between the first two cards. A one-card spread [Jack-King] pays off at 5 to 1. A two-card spread [Jack-Ace] pays off at 4 to 1. A three-card spread [Ten-Ace] pays off at the rate of 2 to 1, and any spread higher than three pays off at even money. If you need clarification on this, the Jack-Ace creates a 2-card spread because there are only two cards which fall between a Jack and an Ace, namely the King and the Queen. The dealer always announces the size of the spread, gives you a moment to decide whether to double your wager, and then deals the third card.

To keep yourself out of trouble in this game, study the chart in Figure 1 while keeping in mind the payoffs listed above. Those of you who are interested can determine the house edge on your own. I'll merely state that it is very high. Yes, you do benefit by being able to double your wager in favorable situations, but even if you cut the house edge in half, you're still better off playing Roulette. However, this is another one of those games which can be fun to play, so at least give yourself a chance by studying this chart.

Figure 1

Spread	Win %	Lose %	True Odds
0	4%	96%	24-1
1	8%	92%	11.5-1
2	16%	84%	5.25-1
3	24%	76%	3-1
4	32%	68%	2-1
5	40%	60%	1.5-1
6	48%	52%	1-1
7	52%	48%	1-1
8	60%	40%	1-1.5

Here is how I came up with these figures. Consider a spread of 4. The first two cards are a Seven and a Queen. We determine the odds by thinking of this as a one-deck game in which only two cards have been dealt. Starting with 52 cards in the deck, we now have only 50 left because one of the Sevens and one of the Queens have already been played. We must draw either an Eight, a Nine, a Ten or a Jack to be a winner. There are four of each of these cards in the deck, so there are 16 total chances of us winning. All of the rest of the cards in the deck will cause us to lose, so we have 34 chances of losing. The number of winning chances divided by the total number of chances [16 divided by 50], gives us our percentage of winning. The ratio of winning chances [16] to losing chances [34] can be determined by dividing 16 into 34, for a result of 2.13, which I listed as 2 in the chart, or odds of 2-1.

It does not take a superior intellect to figure out that your best chances of winning and collecting on proper odds is when the spread is at least 6. Whenever you have a spread of 6 or more, you should definitely double your bet.

I am sure that some of you are thinking that those of us who can count cards should have an easy time of it in this game. After all, if we know that a high number of ten-value cards have been played, and we have a spread that needs a ten-value card, we should not double our wager. Conversely, when we have a spread of only 3 or 4 which requires a ten-value, we may want to double if the shoe is abundant with ten-values, even though the chart indicates the odds are against us. So, yes, counting can definitely help.

Unfortunately, since the spread changes on every hand, and since the exact cards required also changes, counting cards does not help as much as you would hope. For example, a spread of 4 on this hand could be Six-Jack, then on the next hand it might be Two-Seven, and then again it might be Nine-Ace. Counting cards might aid us in the case of the Two-Seven hand or the Nine-Ace hand, but the Six-Jack hand is still up for grabs.

The real key to this game is to know what the spread will be before you make your initial bet. I suppose a really good counting system would help solve this problem, but I have yet to discover it. I hope you do. Until then, keep your wagers at the minimum and double only when the odds are on your side. Losing $$ is one thing, donating it is another.

Chapter 10

Sports Book /
Sports Betting

There is no question that betting on sporting events generates more interest and more wagering activity than any other gambling venue. For some reason, a lot of us cannot tolerate watching a sporting event unless we have some "action", a wager to make the contest just a little more interesting. Of course the amount which is illegally wagered in America greatly exceeds the amount which is legally wagered, but should you find yourself in Nevada at a Sports Book, you can make a legal bet. And not only can you make a legal wager, you can do so in very plush surroundings. Most all of the Sports Books offer a large screen television, and many of them have numerous large screen televisions, while virtually all of them have numerous small screen televisions. Nearly all Sports Books have comfortable seating, comparable to the best types of theater or auditorium seating, some with tablet arms for writing and figuring, most with tables, and some of them even have small-screen televisions at each seat. The only time you need to move is when you get up to make a wager, but I'm sure this will soon change so that you'll be able to wager from your seat. Should the present trends continue, I wouldn't be surprised to find leather recliners instead of chairs in our future, each connected via computer to the Sports Books' computers and our credit card companies.

From any seat in the Sports Book, on most any given day, via satellite, you may be able to watch thoroughbred racing from New York, harness racing from Chicago, quarter horses sprinting in California, and even greyhounds competing in Arizona or Oregon. If you happen to be there on a Saturday, you may be able to see all of the above, plus a minimum of four or five different college football or basketball games, all at the same time! You'll also see huge display boards with the names and associated odds or point spreads for all of the contests for which the Sports Book is accepting wagers. The display board may take up an entire wall a hundred feet tall or even higher, and be several hundred feet wide. It may look like a theater marquee, or be completely electronic with brilliant colors flashing all sorts of information. As in the regular casino, there will be attractive waitresses to fetch your drinks, and sometimes food, and at the very least there will usually be a hot dog or deli stand which can serve up your favorite dog or corned beef sandwich without causing you to miss more than a minute from the action. [I must point out here that the very best sandwiches, and especially hot dogs, are usually found in or adjacent to the Sports Book at most casinos. I often find myself lunching in the Sports Book environment, even if I don't have a wager working.]

We'll assume that you want to get away from the Blackjack or Craps tables for awhile, or that one of your favorite teams is playing, or that you simply want to experience a Sports Book. Let's further assume that while in the Sports Book, you talk yourself into making a small wager. What are the important things you must know? Actually, very little. You must know how a "Point Spread" works, and you must know how to interpret the "line" or "odds" involved in betting each event. Since the most popular sports, in terms of betting activity, are football and basketball, both college and professional, I'll start with the Point Spread.

Read any major metropolitan newspaper during the football season and you will find, normally at the back of the sports section, a listing of all the major college and professional games which are to be played during that particular week. A typical example might look like this:

Favorite	Points	Underdog
DENVER	7	Chicago
Houston	3	SAN FRANCISCO
NEW ORLEANS	4	Buffalo

This information is interpreted thusly: The Denver Broncos are picked to beat the Chicago Bears by 7 points. The "line" on the game is that Denver is favored by 7 points. Since DENVER is typed in bold caps, this means they are the home team. Houston, playing at San Francisco, is a 3 point favorite, and New Orleans, playing at home, is a 4 point favorite against Buffalo.

In the Sports Book, the large display boards you see behind the wagering counter would reflect the "line", or Point Spreads, by noting the same information like this:

> Broncos -7   Bears +7
> 49ers   +3   Oilers -3
> Saints   -4   Bills +4

Being a fan of the Chicago Bears, I might be interested in wagering, say $50 that the Bears will beat the points in this game. Please note that I said I am willing to wager that the Bears will "beat the points in this game". I did not say the Bears were going to "win" this game. This is because it is not necessary for the Bears to win the game in order for me to win my bet. I am not betting that the Bears will win, I am betting that *either* the Bears will win the game outright, or that should they lose, they will lose by less than 7 points. The +7 behind the Bears name means that when the game is over, for the purposes of my bet, I am going to add 7 points to the final score for the Bears, and that will determine the outcome of my bet. When there is a + "plus" sign behind the team you want to bet, it means that you are "taking" the points. Conversely, a - "minus" sign behind the team you want to bet would mean that you are "giving" the points. To make this wager, I simply walk up to the counter in the Sports Book, give the "teller" my money, and say something like "I'll take the Bears and the seven points." I could also say, "I want the Bears," or any words to that effect.

Using the Broncos and Bears as our example, if the actual final score of this game is Broncos 17, Bears 6, the score after adjusting for the points would depend on whether you bet on the Broncos or Bears. If you took the Broncos, you were "giving" 7 points, which means you must subtract 7 points from their score, making the score for your bet Broncos 10, Bears 6. Obviously, you won. On the other hand, let's say you bet on the Bears, and were therefore "taking" the 7 points, which means you must add 7 points to their score. In this scenario, the final score for purposes of your wager was Broncos 17, Bears 13, and you lost.

Are you with me on this? What if the actual final score was, say, Broncos 12, Bears 6, and you bet the Bears? Did the Bears win? Did you win your bet? Which is more important? The answers: No. Yes. Winning the bet.

Remember that the Point Spread has no effect on the actual final score of the game. The Broncos won this game by the score as listed, 12 to 6. Fortunately, for us, we were "taking" 7 points with our bet on the Bears, so the final score for our bet was Broncos 12, Bears 13. We win the bet. To address the last question, if you still feel good when the Bears win but you lose money, there is definitely something wrong with you. You obviously should not be making any wagers, unless someone is willing to bet you utilizing bottle caps or paper clips as tender instead of real money. On the other hand, if you can be happy when you win your bet, even though the Bears lose, you are a normal, well-adjusted American gambler.

One more example: the actual final score is Broncos 13, Bears 6. You took the Broncos, thereby "giving" the 7 points. Who won the game? Who won the bet?

Well, if you were giving 7 points away, the score for your bet is Broncos 6, Bears 6. The Broncos won the game, but nobody won the bet. The bet is a tie or push and nobody wins, nobody loses.

So now we all understand the Point Spread. But you must also know about that $50 I was going to wager. Because, you see, the Sports Book is not in business merely to supply all of us with plush surroundings and a good time. It is in business to make money. Can you actually bet $50 to win $50? No. Think of it this way: In our example, what would happen if exactly 1,000 people bet $50 on the Bears, and exactly 1,000 people bet $50 on the Broncos? The answer is either 1,000 people will be happy, in the case of either team winning with the point spread, or that nobody will be happy, in the case of a tie with the point spread, but for sure the Sports Books *would not* be happy because regardless of what happens, they cannot possibly make any money. $50,000 was wagered on the Bears, the same $50,000 on the Broncos, so the Sports

Book was holding $100,000. Regardless of who wins, they must pay out the same $100,000. In the event of a tie, they must return all bets; therefore, they make no money.

How does the Sports Book make their money? All bets are made based on odds of 11 to 10. If you make a bet of $11 and win, you win $10. Your $11 is returned to you, along with the $10 in winnings. We were going to make a bet of $50, remember? Well, we can't do that, because all bets are made in multiples of 11. Consequently, our bet should be $55, which will pay us $50 when we win [actually, we will collect $105, which represents our bet of $55, plus our winnings of $50]. A wager of $66 would pay $60, a wager of $22 would pay $20, a wager of $1,100 would pay $1,000, a wager of $770 would pay $700, etc.

Think again about our example where 1,000 people each bet $50 on the Broncos, and another 1,000 bet the Bears for the same amount. Well, we now see that all of those people would really bet $55 each, so the Sports Book is holding a total of $110,000 [$55,000 + $55,000]. The final score of the game is Broncos 10, Bears 7. All of us Bear supporters won our bet, because the score for our bet is Broncos 10, Bears 14, and all of us who bet $55 are about to have that $55 returned to us, along with another $50 in winnings, so we are going to collect a total of $105. Since there are 1,000 of us who were smart enough to take the points and the Bears, the Sports Book will need to pay out $105 X 1,000 bettors = $105,000. How much were they holding? $110,000. What is their profit? $5,000. And this, folks, is how the Sports Book makes their money. However, you say, what if the game, for purposes of the bets, is a tie? Well, nobody wins, nobody loses, and the Sports Book makes no money [also known as vigorish]. This very seldom happens, and the reason it seldom happens is because every football game ever played will end in a score which involves a whole number. Scores like 10 to 3, 15 to 6, or 78 to 34. But, while the Sports Books will post point spreads of whole numbers as I did in our example, they will also quite often use a point spread which includes one half of a point [1/2]. In our examples of how the point spreads would look on the boards at the Sports Book, they might also look like this:

Broncos	-7 1/2	Bears	+7 1/2
49ers	+3	Oilers	-3
Saints	-4 1/2	Bills	+4 1/2

With a point spread that includes a number which is not whole, there can be no ties, insuring that the Sports Book will make the vigorish regardless of the outcome.

This knowledge regarding the Point Spread is all you need to know to make your bet. However, it is interesting to note that the Point Spread is not pulled from some crystal ball, nor based on what any experts feel will really be the final score. Each Sports Book relies on an expert who supplies their answer to this question: At what Point Spread can we ensure that we will receive an equal amount of wagering on both sides of the contest? Stated in other words, the question would read: At what Point Spread can we ensure that $100,000 is wagered on the Broncos, and $100,000 is also wagered on the Bears? What Point Spread will make all the Bear lovers say to themselves, "I love this spread", while also making all the Bronco lovers say to themselves, "I can't lose with a spread like this."

The expert decides, and these people are unbelievably good at this, that the Broncos should be favored by 8 points. If all the action the Sports Book receives on the game is being placed on the Bears, the Sports Book must decide if the "line" or Point Spread needs to be changed, or "moved". So they change it to 7 points, and note that more people start taking the Broncos. But they prefer not to use a whole number in the Point Spread, so they make it 7 1/2 and at that point they begin receiving balanced betting on both sides. The line stays at 7 1/2 for the rest of the week. Remember that the expert who came up with this line may really think that the Bears are going to kill the Broncos by at least 37 points, but that is not the issue here. The issue is what Point Spread will bring even wagering on both sides, thereby ensuring that the Sports Book protects itself. If the Sports Book received $110,000 from people betting the Bears, and only $11,000 from people betting the Broncos, they would be frantic. They would have collected a total of $121,000, and if the Bears won the bet they would have to pay out a total of $210,000, for a very terrible net loss to the Sports Book of $89,000. Needless to say, the Sports Book would move the line, and keep moving it until the amount of wagers on both sides began to even out. This is why the serious bettor will always shop around for the best Point Spreads; they are not always the same at all Sports Books.

Next, we need to understand how to wager on events which are not listed by Point Spreads. These other events are ordinarily posted according to Odds.

Have you ever heard anyone say something like "I wanted the Cubs over the Cardinals, so I had to bet 8 for 5"? What did this mean? Well, it's actually fairly simple, at least at first. What this means is that the odds are 8 to 5, which means that if you bet on the favorite, [in this case the Cubs], you must bet $8.00 to win $5.00. This also means that some expert who is employed by the Sports Book has decided that if the Cubs and Cardinals meet 13 times during the season, the team he has established as the favorite [the Cubs] should win 8 of those contests.

Does this mean the odds shown on those large white boards will read Cubs 8, Cardinals 5? No. If it reads like that, some people might think they are looking at Point Spreads. Even though you might see numbers like that in your local paper, you will not see them posted in this manner at the Sports Book. Odds at the Sports Books will be posted based on wagers which will produce a winning amount of $100. Our odds on the Cubs and Cardinals of 8 to 5, would have to be changed to an expression of 100, so we must multiply both sides by 20, which means we really have odds of 160 to 100. Yes, this means that a bet of $160 would win $100 if you bet on the Cubs and they win. You heard me right, the Cubs *must* win in order for you to win your bet. When making a bet based on odds, you do not get any help with points. The outcome of your bet is based on the real outcome of the game in question.

Do odds of 160 to 100 mean that you must bet this much? No. I don't mean to confuse you, but odds of 160 to 100 mean that you can bet any amount which is a multiple of the odds as stated. So even though I said we had to convert our 8 to 5 odds to an expression of 100, you can actually bet 8 to win 5, or you could bet 16 to win 10, or 40 to win 25, or any other number which is a multiple of the odds. A simple way to figure this out is to add a decimal point to the odds. 160 to 100 then becomes 1.60 to 1.00, or $1.60 to $1.00. You must bet $1.60 for every $1.00 you want to win. Again, the first number in the odds represents the amount you must wager on the favorite to win a certain amount [160 to 100]. In the Sports Book the large whiteboards would show Cubs - 160.

Fine, you say. Now I have some idea of what the odds mean if I want to bet on the favorite. But what if I want to bet on the underdog

["dog"]? Do odds of 160 to 100 mean that if I want the dog I can bet $100 to win $160? Absolutely not.

Think again in terms of the Sports Book and how they make their money. Using the Cubs and Cardinals at odds of 160 to 100, what if, to keep it very simple, one person bet on the Cubs, and one person on the Cardinals? The Sports Book would then be holding a total of $260. If the Cubs win, they would then need to return that person's $160 wager, plus that person's $100 in winnings, so they would pay back $260, and since they only collected $260, they don't make any money. If the Cardinals win, they still need to return a total of $260, and still don't make any money. Is the Sports Book in business to make money? You bet. So what happens when someone like you wants to bet the dog?

Look again at the odds board. What it will show you is something like this:

Cubs -160   Cardinals +120

What you see is only one number of the odds. The -160 for the Cubs means that they are the favorites and the odds are 160 to 100. The +120 for the Cardinals means that they are the dog and the odds are 100 to 120. That's right, if you want the Cardinals, you will win $120 for every $100 you wager. Sounds better, doesn't it? If you take the Cardinals you win more than you bet. If you take the Cubs, you win less than you bet. But don't forget that the Cubs should win 8 out of every 13 contests between these two teams. Betting the dog gives you a much better return on your investment, but you may not win a very high percentage of your bets.

Now let's consider the Sports Books' position again. One person bets on the Cubs, one on the Cardinals. The Sports Book is holding $260 [160 + 100]. The Cubs win. The person who bet the Cubs collects back his bet of $160 plus his winnings of $100 for a total of $260. The Sports Book makes no money.

Change the result. The Cardinals win. The person who bet the Cardinals collects back her bet of $100 plus winnings of $120, for a total of $220. The Sports Book just made a profit of $40.

That's right, when the favorite wins the Sports Book breaks even, when the dog wins the Sports Book makes money. The only thing wrong with my example is that the spread between 160 and 120 is a difference of 40, which you may never see in your life. I used a wide spread to clearly illustrate what we're talking about. In the real world, you will seldom see a difference of more than 15 or 20, and a difference of 10 [also known as a "dime line"] is the most prevalent of all.

The house edge on Odds bets starts at about 2% for a dime line, and goes up quickly, so an Odds bet in the Sports Book can be a good one in terms of your disadvantage. Typical odds which you will see posted would look like this:

Cubs   -160   Cardinals +150
Mets   -130   Padres   +120
Red Sox -130   Padres   +115

Once you understand Point Spreads and Odds, you can have a try at the Sports Book. You will probably enjoy the surroundings, and for those of you who prefer to watch television this may be the best place in the casino. You can sit there all day, be entertained, and not wager a penny. But why do that? Didn't you come here to gamble in the first place?

Other items to consider at the Sports Book:

1) When you're betting the horses or dogs, your winning wagers are based on the odds which are posted at the track you are betting. If the odds on your horse at Sportsman Park in Chicago are 7 to 1, and the horse wins and pays $16.40 to the bettors in Chicago, you will receive the same $16.40. If the Exacta pays $56.80 in Chicago, that's what you get.

2) Don't lose your tickets! When you make a bet at the Sports Book you will receive a piece of paper called a ticket which will show exactly how you wagered [Win, Place, Show, Chicago, San Francisco, etc.], and the amount of your wager. To collect a winning bet, you must present your ticket. It's no different than at your favorite horse track. Lose, or for that matter destroy your ticket, and you are out of luck. At most Nevada Sports Books your tickets are good for up to a year, and some Sports Books will even cash your ticket by mail. If you misplace a ticket and find it nine months later, there is an excellent chance it is still collectable.

3) You will find that there are numerous types of wagers which can be made at a Sports Book. I call these wagers "crazy" bets, because, you guessed it, anybody who makes these bets with any frequency is a real loony toon. I am referring to bets like Parleys, Half Time Bets, Teasers, and Totals. If you want to bet a Parley for $5, it may be worth a try because you could get very lucky. If you want to bet a Parley for $500 you need to talk to a shrink. This is like playing the slot machines. The odds are stacked against you, but it can still be fun to play so long as you are not playing with any of your "serious" gambling money.

◆

Chapter 11

Slot Machines/ Video Poker

Consider this proposition: You give me a dollar and I'll give you ninety cents. No deal, you say?

Okay, let me try another one: You give me $100 and I'll give you $90. Not just once. We'll make this exchange, your $100 for my $90, a hundred times a day. Still no deal? Well, let me sweeten the pot. You give me $100 and I'll give you $90 a hundred times each day for six days, and then on the seventh day of each week I'll give *you* $100 for every $80 you give me. Sound better? No, not really. If you were to agree to this proposition and try it for one week, I'd be $4000 ahead of you. I'd give you a total of $64,000 and you'd give me a total of $68,000. That is *not* a good deal.

Yet that is exactly how slot machines work. For every dollar put in them, they give back about ninety-five cents. That is, *some* of them give back ninety-five cents. Some slot machines only return seventy or eighty cents for each dollar.

Would any intelligent person play a game in which the casino's advantage could be 20% or more? Remember Baccarat? A bet on Banker's gives the casino an advantage of only 1.2%. Comparing a bet on Banker's to playing slot machines, your chances of winning are nearly seventeen times greater at Baccarat! A bet on the Pass Line in Craps has over fourteen times greater chance of winning than a bet in a slot machine. So, the question becomes, why do people play slot machines?

Well, you know the answer as well as I do. People play slot machines because they are fun, addictive, and offer huge payoffs. Even though you know it's highly unlikely that you'll win, even though you know you're *donating* money to the casino, you still play the metal monsters.

Since slot machines take up a large share of each casino's gaming area, I won't spend any time describing them. When you enter a casino, you can't possibly miss them. Most of them can be played for nickels, dimes, quarters, half-dollars, and dollars. Some of the newer machines require five dollars, twenty-five dollars, or even, for those high rollers, one hundred dollars for each pull of the handle.

To play a slot machine, you insert the coin or coins required and either pull the lever usually found on the right side of the machine, or push a button on the machine's chest usually marked "Spin". Some machines have only three reels (also called columns or wheels), others have four or five. When you pull the handle, the reels spin and then stop one at a time. If you hit a winning combination, the machine spits your winnings into a metal catcher at the bottom of the machine, bells start ringing, lights flash, and sometimes sirens blare.

A list of all possible winning combinations can be found on the machine's chest. Each reel normally contains twenty symbols: bars, 7's, $'s, diamond symbols, and so forth. A machine might pay, for example, two coins if the first reel is a cherry, or five if the first *two* reels are cherries, or thirty coins if the *three* reels are all bars. The machines seldom make mistakes on payoffs, but make sure you know all the winning combinations. More than one person has overlooked a winner which was not paid correctly.

Also, jackpots (the largest payoff given by the machine) are not normally paid entirely by the machine. If you hit a $1,000 jackpot the machine will only pay a small portion, the rest to be paid by an attendant. If you ever have the good fortune to hit a jackpot, *do not* play the machine again until *after* you have received your total prize. The machines are supposed to "freeze" until an attendant pays you off and releases it, but why take any chances? If you hit a jackpot *do not* leave the machine. Call for an attendant, scream for help, yell until you're hoarse, but do not leave the machine. The casino won't try to cheat you, but other gamblers might.

I once observed two women playing five machines each. Both would start at one slot machine, insert their coins, pull the handle and move on to the next machine with the reels of the first still spinning. Then each of them would start all over again, moving from machine to machine as though working on an automotive assembly line in Detroit. This is not an uncommon sight, but what happened that day was unusual.

Both women were playing machines on the same side of the aisle. You guessed it. A machine in the middle hit the jackpot of $1,250. Can you guess what ensued? Right! Each woman claimed she'd been playing that machine.

The disagreement started politely enough, then escalated to a shoving and shouting match. Ever seen two sixty-year-old women try to clobber each other? The confrontation was amusing to watch while it was verbal, dismal to see after one woman slapped the other. Both were hauled away by security guards. I hope that one of them collected that jackpot. I'm sure both of them truly believed the *other* was cheating.

Most of us fool around with slot machines in hope of hitting the jackpot. But what are your chances of this happening? Consider the following: If a slot machine has three reels, each with twenty symbols, there are 8,000 possible combinations (20 x 20 x 20). And only *one* of those combinations will win the jackpot. If it is a dollar machine with a $1,500 jackpot, $8,000 could go into it before some lucky person wins the $1,500.

The next time you play a slot machine, remember the following:

1) If a machine has three reels, your odds of hitting the jackpot are 8,000 to 1.
2) If a machine has four reels, your odds of hitting the jackpot are 160,000 to 1.
3) If a machine has five reels, your odds of hitting the jackpot are 3,200,000 to 1.

Are the odds really that bad? Yes. But, you ask, does that mean I'd have to put $8,000 into a three-reel machine just to win $1,500? No. The reasons are twofold:

1) When you play a three-reel slot machine you don't know if your coin is the *first* to be inserted into that machine or the *7,999th* coin to be inserted.

2) If the machine is set to pay back 80% of the money put into it, you should receive many small payoffs before hitting the jackpot. You still might have to pull the handle 8,000 times, but it wouldn't cost you $8,000.

Let's explore this further. I'll assume that you're playing a three-reel, dollar machine. The reason you're playing that particular machine is because you saw a sign in front of the casino which stated, "Our $1 Slots Pay 97%". You interpret the sign to mean that if you put in $100 you'll get back at least $97. Well, you could be right, you could be wrong. Your first coin could win the jackpot, your tenth coin could win the jackpot, any of your coins could win smaller payoffs, or perhaps *none* of your coins will win anything.

If this dollar machine really pays back 97%, out of every $8,000 put into it $7,760 will be returned to the players. In other words, the machine will only retain $240. But *whose* $240 will it retain? Yours? The next player's? Who knows? It may very well take $100 of your money and only give back $10. Then, for the very next person to play the machine, it may give back $30 for $1. There is no way to tell who the machine will pay. And it's even worse than I've described. The machine may keep $3,000 before returning *any* money. I once interviewed an attendant who had been watching one particular dollar machine for the entire four months of his tenure. During that time the machine had *never* paid a jackpot even though it had been in continuous use.

Instead of thinking about what a 97% machine might mean to *you*, think about what it means to the casino. If that machine is played 8,000 times each week (which is *very* possible), the casino will net $240 per week. That's $1,040 per month, $12,480 per year. If the casino had fifty such machines (again, *very* possible), the casino would net $619,200 each year! If the payoff rate was 90% instead of 97%, which is more than likely, it would net $2,064,000 per year. And if the payoff rate was 80% it would net $4,128,000 each year. Is it any wonder why casinos have so many slot machines? Would you like to have five or ten of them in your basement?

VIDEO POKER

Another form of slot is the Video Poker machines which have grown astronomically in popularity. And while they take more than merely a simple pull of the handle to play, they are *still* a form of slot machine. They are preset to return to the players a certain fixed percentage of all the monies they accept. This preset percentage could be anywhere from about 75% to nearly 99%.

To play them with any hope for success, you *must* know and understand the ranking of Poker hands and the basics of playing five-card draw. With Video Poker you feed your coins into the little monster and are dealt five cards, all face up. You can then hold or discard anywhere from none to all of them, and the machine will deliver new cards to replace your discards. Depending on the type of machine being played, you normally need to finish the hand with at least a pair of Jacks to collect any coins.

It is not my intent to teach you how to play Video Poker, what to hold and draw, etc. For detailed information, visit your local bookstore and purchase any one of the numerous books devoted entirely to Video Poker. However, I will emphasize three important facts on the subject:

1) The maximum payoff on a Video Poker machine is paid when the player achieves a hand consisting of a Royal Flush. The odds of catching or drawing one of these hands is roughly 40,000 to 1. (Yes, this is different than real Poker, and that's because the machines have computer chips which are programmed to produce more winning hands than you would see in real Poker.) The payoff if you hit a Royal Flush on a dollar machine with the maximum of five coins played, is typically $4,000. Do you see a casino advantage here? Well, it's not as bad as it sounds, because the machine will make thousands of smaller payoffs during the time it takes to deliver that Royal Flush.

2) In my opinion, Video Poker machines are much more fun to play because of the fact that you must make decisions.Any idiot can pull a handle or punch a button and play a slot machine. Any idiot can also play a Video Poker machine. However, with Video Poker, the more intelligent your decisions, the greater your chance of winning.

3) Video Poker is by far the most popular game currently offered by the casinos of America. If the casinos had their choice, they would eliminate all table games and replace them with V.P. machines. Can you blame them? Low maintenance, high degree of popularity, and a locked-in guarantee of profits.

MONEY MANAGEMENT

In the introduction to this book, I suggested that no more than 20% of your gambling funds should be used as fun money. I now suggest that 50% of your 20% can be used for slot machines and Video Poker. If your fun money is $200, don't risk more than $100. I know that doesn't sound like much money, but it is equivalent to 400 quarters. $100 on nickel machines could give you 2,000 pulls of the handle, and the rate of payoffs on the nickel machines is as good as any, the jackpots still in proportion to the more expensive machines. Whether you win $200 on a nickel machine or $1,200 on a dollar machine, the ratio is the same. The dollar machine just costs a lot more to play.

Another suggestion: On most machines you can play from one to five coins on each pull, the payoff increasing for each coin; a one-coin jackpot might be $200, a two-coin jackpot $400, a three-coin jackpot $1,000, etc. On those machines it is in your best interest to always play maximum coins on each pull. If you can't afford to play maximum coins on a $1 machine, play with quarters. If betting $1.25 (five coins) is still too steep, drop back to nickels. The machines do not care how many coins have been played. In Video Poker, for example, that machine is going to produce a Royal Flush every 40,000 hands regardless of whether one or five coins have been played. Consequently, if you hit one with only one coin in, you have just stolen from the rest of us who always play five coins. The casino, however, is delighted with you because the one-coin payoff is peanuts.

Also, when playing either the slots or Video Poker, make sure that the machine accepts your coin or coins *before* you pull any handles or press any buttons. Sometimes, your coins can pass through the machine and drop in the metal catcher. I once hit a jackpot while playing a three-coin machine. Unfortunately, only one of my three coins had been accepted by the machine, but I hadn't noticed. My jackpot paid at the one-coin rate of $200. Had all three of my coins been accepted, the payoff would have been $1,000! My lack of attention cost me $800.

Have fun with slot machines and Video Poker. Just don't expect to win a lot money.

Chapter 12

1	2	3	4	5	6	7	8	9	10
11	12	13	14	15	16	17	18	19	20
21	22	23	24	25	26	27	28	29	30
31	32	33	34	35	36	37	38	39	40

Keno

As an experiment, I once asked ten random gamblers to describe the game of Keno. All of them began by pointing out that Keno was very similar to Bingo. Both are played with numbered cards and with Ping-Pong balls drawn from a machine. Bingo has 75 numbers, Keno has 80. Yet, Keno and Bingo are *not* similar.

In Bingo, numbers are drawn until someone wins. If it takes 65 numbers to produce a winner, then 65 numbers are drawn. There is a winner in every game.

In Keno, only *20* numbers are drawn, and it is quite possible that a game will have *no* winners.

To play Keno, you must first obtain a Keno card (ticket). You will find these at the Keno counter, in the Keno lounge, and in most of the casino's bars and restaurants. The tickets are free and easily found. You then select, depending on how you want to play, anywhere from one to twenty of your favorite numbers. If some or all of your numbers are drawn from the Keno blower in the next game, you could win anything from even money to $50,000. Figure 1 shows a Keno ticket played for $10 with one number selected. In addition to checking the numbers you desire, you must also indicate on the ticket how many numbers you are playing and how much money you are wagering.

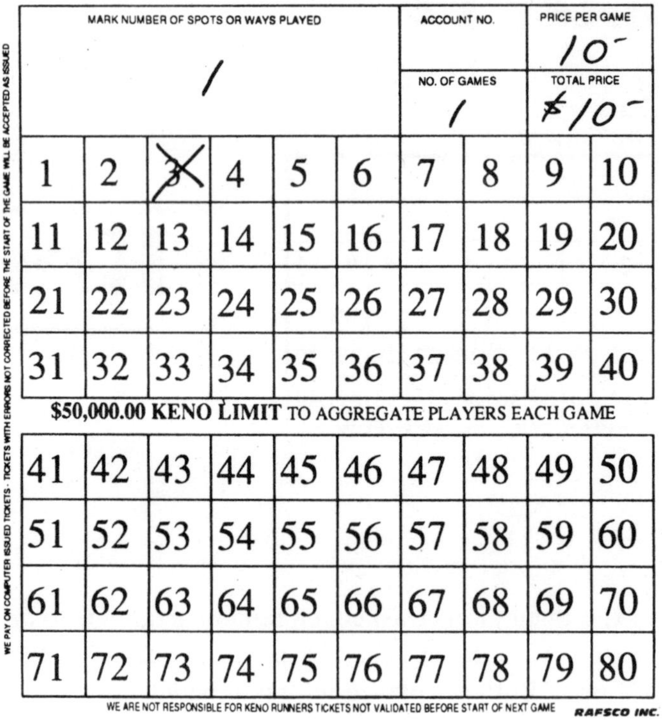

Figure 1

After filling out the ticket you take it to the Keno counter, hand over your wager, and receive an authorized copy of your ticket with the game number noted in the upper right corner.

Figure 2 shows what your authorized copy will look like. If you're sitting in a bar or restaurant, you can also have a Keno runner take your ticket and money to the Keno counter. Runners are men and women who dress like waiters but actually work the Keno game. You'll see them working various areas by calling out: "Keno?", "Keno?", which is their way of asking whether you have a ticket for them to pick up. Normally, these runners are very reliable. However, you should know that if the runner doesn't get your ticket back to the counter in time for the next game, or if they make some sort of mistake, the casino is not responsible for them.

				GREEN GAME	FIRST GAME 177		NO. OF GAMES	PRICE	

| | | | | | LAST GAME 177 | 1 | | $10.00 | |

LIMITS AS POSTED IN KENO PAY BOOKS

1	2	3	4	5	6	7	8	9	10	1/1 10.00
11	12	13	14	15	16	17	18	19	20	
21	22	23	24	25	26	27	28	29	30	
31	32	33	34	35	36	37	38	39	40	

KENO RULES ON THE BACK OF THIS TICKET

41	42	43	44	45	46	47	48	49	50
51	52	53	54	55	56	57	58	59	60
61	62	63	64	65	66	67	68	69	70
71	72	73	74	75	76	77	78	79	80

22NOV98 ᴰᴬᵀᴱ   13:36   326   3-0467

Figure 2

Once you've paid for your ticket and received your authorized copy there is nothing to do but sit back and relax. You have no control over the game. Eighty Ping-Pong balls will decide your fate.

As the numbers are drawn from the Keno blower they are flashed onto Keno boards which are located throughout the casino. Whether you win depends on how many of your selected numbers are drawn. For your eight number ticket, typical payoffs are shown in Figure 3.

CATCH	BET $1	BET $2	BET $5
5 Win	$9	$18	$45
6 Win	$90	$180	$450
7 Win	$1,495	$2,990	$7,475
8 Win	$25,000	$50,000	$50,000

Figure 3

If six of your numbers were drawn, you would win a $90 payoff for your $1 bet. Sound good? Had all eight of your numbers been drawn you would win $18,000 for your $1 bet. Sound even better?

Obviously, the Keno payoffs supply all the attraction anyone needs to play the game. However, when you consider your chance of actually winning, this game is even worse than slot machines. After studying Figure 4 I am sure you will think my statistics must be wrong, that the odds could not possibly be this bad. Well, guess again.

IF YOU SELECT	THE ODDS OF ALL YOUR NUMBERS BEING DRAWN ARE
1 Number	4-1
2 Numbers	17-1
3 Numbers	72-1
4 Numbers	326-1
5 Numbers	1,550-1
6 Numbers	7,755-1
7 Numbers	40,843-1
8 Numbers	230,230-1
9 Numbers	1,381,380-1
10 Numbers	8,909,900-1
11 Numbers plus	. . .it just gets worse

Figure 4

No, you did not read it wrong. If you select ten numbers on your Keno ticket, the chance of all ten numbers being drawn is roughly one in nine million. Yes, you're probably better off trying to win a state lottery.

The casino's advantage is difficult to determine in this game, but the smallest advantage is about 25% on a one-number ticket, and obviously runs well over 100% on other wagers.

However, there is always the chance that your ten-number ticket is the one out of nine million. And if that happened, wouldn't you expect a payoff larger than $50,000? Well, sorry, because that's the max you can collect no matter if it's a dollar ticket or a twenty-dollar ticket. Of course there is also the possibility that six of your ten numbers might show up, or seven out of ten, etc. Don't count on it. The odds are still so bad that you would have a better chance of striking oil in your back yard. If you are willing to play a ten-number ticket nine million times in order to hit a $50,0000 payoff, perhaps I can interest you in Colorado pine cones which I am willing to sell for only $5,000 each.

If your ticket does win, you can collect your winnings at the Keno counter or have the Keno runners make the trip for you. Just remember that winning tickets must be collected prior to the start of the next game.

Also note that in most casinos the aggregate payout is a total of $50,000. This means that the total maximum payoff for all winners in any one game is $50,000. If there is more than one winner in a single game, the total payoff to *all* the winners cannot exceed $50,000. So just because you get a $50,000 winner does not mean you will collect $50,000.

Note: Some casinos are now offering versions of Keno which offer payoffs of over $100,000.

MONEY MANAGEMENT

If your vacation is for three days and two nights, you'll probably eat eight meals at your hotel/casino. During the time required to eat each meat, you could play three games of Keno. At $1 per game, that's $24. No, I am not suggesting that you risk $24 on Keno. All I'm saying is that you *could* risk $24. Personally, I think one game per meal is ideal. That's only $8. Any more than that is lunacy. You can't protect your money in games where the casino has *at least* a 25% advantage over the player.

Chapter 13

Junkets

Wanna take a trip to a casino at nearly no cost to you? Wanna have fun for a day? Do you have gambling fever? Will you soon turn into a raving mad-dog killer, alcoholic misfit, or simply a severe grouch if you don't get to roll those bones pretty darn soon? Do you dream of getting Blackjacks on every hand, or of beating the dealer with 15s and 16s? Then you need a fix. And since you can't take time off from work right this minute, we're going to give you a shot of a drug called Junket. What is it? What are the side effects? Read on.

A Junket is simply a quick trip to a casino. They may also be called "excursions" or "charters". By "quick", I mean the trip normally consists of 1-2 days. On a 1-day Junket, you will probably leave your home town by approximately 8:30 in the morning, and return by about 11:00 the same night. Depending upon how far you are from the casino, this will leave you anywhere between nine and thirteen hours of action at the casino. If you need to travel through several time zones to make this trip, you may need to leave earlier in the morning, arrive back later at night, or both. But you will still get in your ten or twelve hours of gambling. On an overnight, 2-day trip, the hours of departure and return may be about the same. The only difference is that you will have a room at the casino/hotel and stay over for one night.

Junkets are sponsored by casinos. The casino will pay some enterprising business person in your area a nominal fee to organize your trip, collect deposits to ensure you make the plane or bus, and keep everybody happy. Some of these business people are associated with travel agencies, most have diverse occupations. The leader of your group may be your next door neighbor, your mailman, your insurance agent, in short, any person interested in making a little money in their spare time. Or, your Junket may be organized by a company which specializes in planning these trips, which is increasingly the case. A company which not only can arrange for you to go to Atlantic City, but can also get you to Elko, Nevada.

The enticing thing about a Junket is that it allows you to make this trip at a cost which is much less than what you would ordinarily expect to pay. In exchange for the reduced cost of the trip, you will be expected to gamble at your sponsoring casino for the entire duration of the trip, often at preset minimum wagers. If, for example, the Golden Pearl Casino is sponsoring the trip, they would not want you to get off the plane and head directly for their hated enemy the Black Fate Saloon and Casino. If that's what you want to do, if you want to "cheat" your host casino, probably the worse thing that will happen is that your host will scream at you a little, and stare at you a lot, and you'll never make another trip with this group. But don't be a jerk about this. If the Golden Pearl is offering a good package, be an honorable person and hold up your end of the bargain. Don't take advantage of a Junket to Carson City, Nevada just because you have an aunt who lives there that you haven't seen in a long time.

Here's a few examples of Junkets which will easily explain their essence.

Wendover, Nevada

This is a destination which is very popular for people living anywhere from Minneapolis to Oakland. The cost of this trip [A.K.A. the reservation fee] is currently $119, though it varies depending on your home city. A modern jet is utilized to transport you back and forth. Prior to boarding the plane you must show your host $500 in cash, proof positive that you at least have the money to gamble, whether you in fact gamble or not. You are expected to play at this particular casino for your entire stay. You are expected to make minimum wagers of $5 at all table games, and minimum bets of five coins if you are playing quarter Video Poker. The group assembles at either the local airport or perhaps the reception room of a small, private aviation company. An assistant to the host checks to make sure that you are on the list, and that you have already paid your reservation fee. You will then be assigned a specific seat on the plane. You will also receive a badge of some sort which you will be expected to have pinned to a conspicuous place on your clothing for the duration of the Junket. This badge will reflect a number associated with your name. This is how the casino keeps track of who you are and whether you are living up to your end of the arrangement. Once you have your seat assignment and your badge, you are also given coupons which are good for free meals, match-play certificates, discounts on merchandise, etc.

Next, you stand around, or sit, and converse with your fellow passengers. Perhaps, if this is your first trip, you may be a little nervous, so you should ask some of the others if they have made this trip before. Some have, and they put your mind at rest by telling you that this is a small, but first-class, casino which makes every effort to ensure that you will enjoy yourself and come back again.

There is a slight delay in your departure time, because the same jet which is delivering you also made a run from another city further East which left earlier this morning, and it encountered strong head winds crossing Utah. This same jet, by the way, may drop off your group and then make another run to some city further west.

Once you've boarded the aircraft, the host makes a short speech telling you what a good time you're going to have. The plane takes off. There are real stewardesses who come around with drinks and a snack, just like on a real commercial airliner. The host organizes a drawing for cash and other prizes, and you put your $1 or $5, or whatever the amount, into the hat in hopes that you'll start the day off lucky.

Several buses are waiting for your group at the Wendover airport. You file off the plane and immediately onto the buses. The ride to the casino takes only five minutes.

You enter the casino, it looks like most nice casinos that you have ever seen before, you play the games of your choice. Later, you check into your room, take a nap, then return to a full night of food, show and gambling. The following morning you enjoy a first-class breakfast buffet, hit the tables again, and before you know it a voice on the public address system is announcing that your bus is now loading and this is the last call. In the meantime, you have met the folks who came in earlier from Omaha, and also those that came in later from Oakland. Whether or not you had a good time may depend upon whether you won or lost money, but you must admit that you were treated fairly by friendly casino employees. This, folks, is a very typical trip.

Elko, Nevada

Basically the same package as the one to Wendover. $59 reservation fee, meal ticket to the buffet, show $350 cash, only $2 minimum table games, $1 minimum slot play. Leave at about 9:00 AM, back home about midnight. For slightly more money, this Junket also offers a one night package, and at times even a two-night package.

Incidentally, some of you may be thinking: "Who in their right mind would even consider making a trip to some place like Elko, Nevada, which can't possibly be more than a tiny pit stop on some two-lane highway out in the middle of the desert?" Some of you may not want to go anywhere except Atlantic City, Las Vegas, or Reno. To those of you who think like that, I say: "Is Florida the only place in the world where you can get sunshine in December?" Of course not! Even though Elko is a small town, the highway is four-lane and major, the casinos have all the class of a Las Vegas strip casino, they are just a tad smaller. So don't turn your nose up at the idea of a Junket just because it's not going to a "major" or "name" destination. Don't ignore blondes just because you know you like redheads.

How did I discover these Junkets? I found most of them advertised in either the travel section of the Sunday newspaper, or in the sports section on most any day. Once you take a trip with a Junket operator, you will automatically be on their mailing list every time they design a new Junket. There are casinos now located throughout the entire United States. For casino action, you no longer need rely only on Nevada or Atlantic City. Where there are casinos, there are Junkets being offered. For example, one company is now offering Junkets to, of all places, Tunica, Mississippi from cities as divest as Indianapolis and Dallas.

If you have a favorite casino, merely inquire with their marketing department as to whether they have Junkets available, from where, at what times, etc.

Chicago to Atlantic City

Your reservation fee starts at about $160, and could go up to about $300 depending on whether you travel during the week or on a weekend [obviously, the amount of the reservation fee would be subject to change if this Junket company is using regular commercial flights]. Like all the others, you depart early AM, return late PM. The rest is slightly different from the trips I described earlier. Instead of charging only a nominal reservation fee, like in Elko, you pay out between $160 and $300. But does the trip really cost you this much? No. Here's why. This Junket returns to you all of the following: $20 in cash, $20 worth of food vouchers, a $20 voucher which can be applied to a future trip, a $15 show and free cocktail, a $10 voucher for the bus trip from and to the airport, and a free gift of unknown value from the casino. If your reservation fee was $120, and you subtract the value of all these bonuses, the actual cost of this trip is only about $35.

Bus From Your East Coast Town to Atlantic City

There are numerous East Coast towns which offer a bus to Atlantic City for a nominal reservation fee. Most of these operate like the trip I described to Elko, except that you are traveling by bus instead of by airplane.

Must your Junket always include a group? No. Though I tend to think of Junkets as group plans, you can also arrange to stay for several days under some plans and basically travel on your own instead of with a group. For example, several casinos are currently offering a Junket whereby you pay for your own airfare, arrive and depart by your own schedule. You must gamble for a certain time period at a certain minimum bet, which qualifies you for some goodies. Naturally, the goodies vary depending on the nature of your wagers. The $5 bettor can qualify for free drinks anywhere in the casino, free shows, free buffet meals, and a cash allowance which will cover the cost of the room. Added together, these perks make the actual cost of the trip the equivalent of the cost of the airfare only. All this $5 bettor must do is play for a minimum of 8 hours during his stay of two or three nights. These perks used to be offered only to high rollers, those being "comped" by the casino. Due to the changing nature of the gambling business, the picture is beginning to look brighter for a lot of us. The casinos are getting a little tired of fighting each other for the true high rollers, and have discovered that their meat and potatoes are provided by gamblers like you and me who arrive with a stake of $1,000 and play hard for a couple of days. They still want the high rollers, but they need you and me to be successful and they are finally giving us access to the type of programs previously reserved only for the person willing to wager $50 and up per hand. Of course us little guys aren't going to get the best of the suites, or the gourmet meals, or preferred seating at the shows, but we can still have a good time.

As you can see by these examples, there are several options available to us that more or less fall into the Junket category. We can make a short trip at very little cost and satisfy our urges to gamble. Are there pitfalls to beware? Just a couple.

The single thing I like the least about a Junket is that I am forced to stay at that one casino regardless of how I am doing. As I have stated earlier in this book, if you are not doing well at one table, move to another. If you are not doing well at one casino, move to another. When on a Junket that may not be easy to do. You can stop gambling, but then it's kind of boring to sit in a casino all day with no action. However, the good news is that on some Junkets you have a choice of more than one casino. This is because in some locations the same company may own more than one casino, and they are happy to let you play at either one.

I don't like 1-day Junkets because I have nowhere to go during the day should I want to take a nap, a swim, or a break of some kind. Yes, I can go to the coffee shop, or in some cases I can go to the Sports Book, but when I am gambling hard I sometimes need a nap, and I don't have anywhere to take one when I am on a Junket of the one-day variety.

Other than the two limitations just mentioned, I hardly recommend that you try a Junket. Perhaps I have been fortunate, but all of the Junkets I've tried have been well organized and honest.

The one thing, however, that you should do is ask a few questions before sending in your reservation fee. What kind of plane is being used? Is the plane supplied by a company licensed to provide these types of flights? What minimum bets are required? What are the Blackjack rules? Single deck, double deck, or shoe? Is there a Poker Room, and does Poker qualify on this trip? Can you be provided with a list of happy prior customers? If not, can the Junket operator have a satisfied customer call you? What provision has been made in case you need to stay overnight due to inclement weather or airplane malfunction? How long has the Junket operator been scheduling trips to this casino? How long has the Junket operator been scheduling trips to any casinos?

I'm sure you get my drift. So, if you need that quick fix, try out a Junket. It could be just the remedy you need.

Chapter 14

Fate, Luck and Intuition

Let me tell you a story. One day a few years ago I decided to visit a local greyhound track for one of my frequent attempts at pari-mutuel wagering. While driving to the track I turned on the radio. The station was conducting a live interview with a popular athlete who is known locally as T.J. I listened for approximately seven minutes, then hit my station selector. What did I hear next? A newsman reading a story that involved this same athlete with the initials T.J., followed by an advertisement for a company whose name starts with the letters T.J. What was the very next billboard I saw adjacent to the highway? An advertisement for the same company whose advertisement is still running on the radio.

Six or seven minutes later I reach the track. I'm arriving late, so it's almost time for the tenth race. I buy a program. What name do I see, a name which because of what I've seen and heard jumps out at me like a jack-in-the-box?

Right! A greyhound whose name starts with the initials T.J. Do I have enough time to study the program before placing a bet? No. Do I decide that all the T.J.s from the last twenty-five minutes are more than coincidence? Of course. So I bet this T.J. dog on top in the trifecta, he wins and keys a payoff of about $900.

Was this just luck on my part? Was it fate? Was it intuition? Probably a little of each.

Obviously this story has nothing to do with casino gambling, but I relate it because it emphasizes the point that I want to make in this chapter, which is this: In addition to having knowledge of basic systems and odds, you must be aware of what is happening to you and around you. What is happening to and around you will provide you with strong clues as to whether luck or fate are on your side, and whether your intuition has taken a winter vacation in Iceland.

You are playing Blackjack. The twenty you receive on your first hand looks great since the dealer is showing a Six. The dealer's down card is a Seven, he hits and gets a Three, hits again and catches a Five. Twenty-one beats twenty. You lose. The dealer had two chances to bust. First when he hit a hard thirteen, again when he hit a hard sixteen.

You play another round. The twenty you receive on this hand looks every bit as good as the twenty on the hand before, but now the dealer is showing a Ten so you don't have quite the confidence you were feeling on the first hand. Your hopes increase when the dealer reveals a Four for a down card, your eyes widen with delight when he draws an Ace, and then you collapse back onto your chair when he hits again and catches a Six. Again, twenty-one beats twenty. Again, you lose. Again, the dealer had to take two hits, either of which could have busted his hand but did not.

You play again. Being the impatient type, you pick up your first card almost before it hits the felt, and it's an Ace. Even better, the second card is a ten-value and you now have Blackjack. So does the dealer. Blackjack ties a Blackjack, so you didn't lose. Maybe you should stick around for another hand.

Are you crazy? What is happening to you? Think about it. You're losing, yes, but how are you losing? You are getting great hands, but not winning with them. Does someone need to smack you over the head? STOP PLAYING! Change tables or change casinos. At times, how you lose is just as, if not more, important than the fact that you lost.

The casino next door smells good when you walk in. You can't identify the odor, but it suits your senses. Maybe things will improve, you think. Well, tough luck. Your first hand of Blackjack is a wonderful combination of a Seven and a King. Not exactly a great hand, and you get that feeling that you have one foot in the grave. The dealer is showing an Ace. You're probably dead meat on this one. What is the dealer's down card? Take that one foot of yours back out of the grave.

The dealer exposes a Five, then draws a Six and a Jack. Your sixteen beats his twenty-two.

That scent you keep sniffing is smelling better all the time. Betting two units becomes a thought that you act on almost before you realize you're doing it. An Eight and a Three show up on your first two cards. The dealer is showing a Four. You begin to lick your lips. Instead of two units, you wish you had bet two hundred units. You double down. The dealer slips you a card face down. An excited, trembling left hand which is connected to your body reaches out to tip it enough for a peek. It's the Two of Clubs, and you feel a sharp pain in your stomach. Now you wish you had stayed with a one unit wager. The dealer exposes a Seven, for a total of eleven, and you are thinking "here we go again, right down the drain", but the dealer's next card is an Ace, then a Three, and whammo, a Ten. Thirteen beats twenty-five. You win. The dealer had three chances to make a hand, but didn't.

What is happening to you? Of course you are winning, but how are you winning? You are winning hands that you should be losing, hands that you will lose the overwhelming majority of the time. Does someone need to smack you over the head and tell you to recognize that this may be the start of something wonderful? That you had better start thinking in terms of jacking up those bets?

Being slightly timid, you stay with only a two unit bet. You are dealt a marvelous fourteen. The dealer is showing a King. The basic system says to hit. You haven't been counting, so you should play the basic system. But, yet, somehow your gut feeling, your intuition tells you to stand. You know it's not a smart play. In fact it's downright ignorant. Except that it works. The dealer has a Five for a down card and draws an Eight. Fourteen beats twenty-three. You win again.

You are convinced that fate or luck is smiling upon you, so you wisely institute a progressive betting system and you do very well. Congratulations! You weren't simply playing, you were also being aware of what was taking place. The winning of hands that you should be losing is one of the strongest indicators of the birth of a winning streak.

On another occasion you are playing Pai Gow Poker. You win the first hand. You lose the second hand. You win the third hand. You lose the fourth hand. You win the fifth hand. You lose the sixth hand. Does anyone see a pattern here? If you experienced a pattern like this, would you be aware enough to recognize it? Would you do anything about it?

Could you maybe bet one unit on the even hands and then boost your bet up to fifteen or twenty units on the odd hands? If a floorman came over to the table and stared at you, would you shrug and tell him that you've been winning every other hand? Why not? It's the truth. The dealer will confirm what you tell the floorman, and you will not have a problem.

Back to Blackjack. You're at third base. With the dealer showing a Six, the she-devil sitting adjacent to you splits a pair of Tens and receives two more. You stand pat on your thirteen. The dealer's down card is an Eight. Either one of the last two cards off the deck would have busted the dealer had this trash bag next to you stayed with her original twenty like she should have. The dealer catches a Seven and everybody at the table loses.

On the next hand the dealer shows a Six. Your total is eleven. The mess next to you has fifteen. Before you can tell her you'll break her fingers if she tries to hit, she busts her hand with a Queen. You still double down and receive the Eight that would have gone to the dealer had EL BIMBO played her hand correctly. The dealer exposes a Jack as his down card, draws a Three, and you're down the tubes again. If this woman doesn't draw, you end up with twenty-one and the dealer busts. Are you aware of what is happening? This is bad luck and perhaps bad fate as well. Move on.

Conversely, what if the person next to you made all these ignorant moves, and you won because of it? Would that be good? Absolutely. Would this be a good sign? Guess for yourself.

Give Craps a try. Bet the Pass Line. The shooter is hot. She tosses a seven on the comeout, then later makes her point of four. However, there is a man at the table who has been tossing, scattering, and just plain dropping chips all over the table. He claims to have a winner on every throw, whether he actually has one or not. He is quite obnoxious. In fact he is skunk-odorous. Before you know it, one of the dealers, the stickman and the boxman are all being called various nasty names by this guy. They are not enchanted by this man's demeanor. You can see their lips tightening, their faces begin to flush. The point is six, the shooters next roll is a seven. The dice move to the next roller, but so long as Mr. Personality continues to give the pit crew a rough time, nobody can make their number.

Keep this in mind. For some reason, whenever one of the players at your table is upsetting the dealer, stickman, or whomever is controlling that particular game, you may as well move along. Be aware of what is happening to and around you.

Given the situation I just described at the Crap table, would you be sharp enough to either 1] leave the table, or 2] start betting the Don't Pass?

Remember that these examples have nothing whatsoever to do with the science of gambling. They have to do with luck, fate and intuition

Here is something which I do out of habit, because I discovered a long time ago that this action helps me. Whenever I change tables, I always take my chips to the cashier's cage, cash them, and buy new chips before I play again. I do this because I observed during one three-night stay that virtually every time I switched tables and played with existing chips, I lost. Every time I switched tables and did not play until after seeing the cashier, I improved. Note that I did not say that I won. I improved my play. I may still have lost, but at a slower rate. Some people might think this is simply pure luck. Others may analyze this and say that the time it takes me to walk to the cashier's cage and then back to the tables gives me time to collect myself before continuing play. Whatever the case, it works for me.

All of us, I am sure, have at least some regard for fate, luck, and intuition. But even if you don't believe in any of the three, doesn't it make sense to be aware of what is happening to and around you? And doesn't it make very good sense to make modifications in your gambling when you notice that certain incidents tend to help or hinder you? Of course it does. Combine awareness with a sound system of play, and you're sure to find that a pleasant fate visits you frequently, that lady luck smiles a little, and that your intuition is more keen.

Chapter 15

Practical Advice

This chapter is a collection of tips which can mean the difference between success and failure in Las Vegas, Atlantic City, Biloxi, or your favorite Indian Reservation. You cannot enter a casino and rely on blind luck to protect your money or make you a winner. Even though blind luck has probably won more money than all the gambling systems combined, blind luck is not consistent. If lady luck is on your side during your next gambling session, you can do everything wrong and still win. But if lady luck deserts you, you must take steps to protect yourself against disastrous losses. You don't want to lose your entire gambling stake in the first few hours of your trip and then spend the rest of your time swearing at yourself. If you follow all the advice contained in this chapter, one of two things will happen:

1) You will substantially reduce your losses.
2) You might even win.

Some of my suggestions have already been covered in earlier chapters, but all warrant repeating.

MONEY MANAGEMENT

1) Divide your gambling fund into two groups. Eighty percent or more should be serious money, twenty percent or less should be fun money.

2) Start with at least fifty units of serious money. One hundred units is ideal.

3) Do not lose more than four units at any table. Change tables before you lose more. If there aren't anymore tables, change casinos. Often, being at a new table or casino will brighten your outlook and sharpen your judgment.

4) If you win as many as six units, do not lose them back.

5) If you win as many as fifteen units, double your unit. Then if you win another fifteen units, double your unit again. Keep doing this so long as you continue winning. It is amazing how quickly your unit can change from $5 to $80 when things are going your way.

6) Do not forget that you are playing for real money, not chips. Each time the dealer collects one of your green chips, you've lost $25. Chips are money!

7) Above all else, do not gamble with money you cannot afford to lose.

BETTING STRATEGY

Remain at a minimum wager until you begin to win. Do not chase good money with bad money. Increasing your bets when you are losing will not change the cards or dice.

Once you find yourself in a position where your winnings total 25 or 30 units, you may want to try a progressive betting system to help maximize your profits. Here's one I happen to like: Start with a minimum wager. If you win, bet the minimum again. If you win again, double your bet. If you win again, collect your winnings but leave out the same bet (double the minimum). If you then win again, double your bet again. After that the process is drag (collect your winnings but not the bet), then press (double your bet), then drag, press, drag, press, until your luck changes. If you lose, go back to the minimum wager and start again.

If you begin with a one-unit wager, your bets would look like this: 1, 1, 2, 2, 4, 4, 8, 8, 16, 16 and so forth. Using this betting system you are trying for three consecutive wins. If you lose the second bet you break even. If you win the second bet, every succeeding bet adds to your profits without jeopardizing any of your gambling stake. The system is designed to take advantage of any hot streaks you encounter, so that you can maximize your winnings.

Of course if you start with a high unit, say $50, and you win several consecutive hands, you quickly exceed the maximum bet allowed at most tables. If this happens, remain at the maximum bet until you lose, then drop back to your previous bet (half the maximum). If you lose again, go all the way back down to the minimum.

Example: Your betting unit is $50. You win the first hand, so you collect your winnings of $50 and leave out your original bet of $50 for the next round. You win again, but this time you press (add your $50 winnings to your original bet of $50) for a total of $100. You win again, so you drag (remove your winnings, but remain with your last bet). You win again, so you press again (add your winnings to your bet), making your new bet $200. If you win again, you drag $200 and leave the bet at $200. Another win would press your wager to $400, where it would stay for two hands. Then you would bet $800 for the next two hands. The next bet would then be $1,600, but if the table limit is $1,000 you would bet that amount. If you lose, you would drop back to $500. Another loss would send you back to the basic unit of $50. Here's a recap of what your bets looked like:

First wager	$50
Second wager	$50
Third wager	$100
Fourth wager	$100
Fifth wager	$200
Sixth wager	$200
Seventh wager	$400
Eight wager	$400
Ninth wager	$800
Tenth wager	$800
Eleventh wager	$1,000
Twelfth wager	$500

Seldom, if ever, will you win so many consecutive hands, but if it happens you should be prepared to take advantage and maximize your profits. In addition, even if you were only to win five or six hands in a row, you've still maximized your winnings and profits.

But, you ask, what happens if I'm playing Blackjack and my sixth hand is a total of 11 and the dealer is showing a Six? Should I double down? Well, this is what I call a pivotal hand. Win it, and you're rolling. Lose it, and you're right back where you started. Part of me says not to double. Why risk losing a good share of the profits I've accumulated so far? Another part of me says to make the gamble. This is, after all, what it's all about. So I would normally go for it. Yet, the smart play is for you not to become overly greedy. The idea of this betting system is to keep playing with the casino's money . . .that is, money which does not come from our gambling stake. Also, remember that I indicated you would not initiate this system until *after* you have already won 25 or 30 units. So, in general, when you're using this type of progressive betting system in Blackjack, forget about doubling down and splitting. Or, go for it. It's up to you.

True story. I once observed my wife winning fifteen consecutive hands of Blackjack. Unfortunately, she refused to increase her wagers. She started with five-dollar bets and ended with five-dollar bets. Had she used this betting system she would have won 127 units instead of 15.

I cannot emphasize this strongly enough. When you are losing, you want to be making minimum wagers. When you are winning, you want to win *multiple* units on each bet.

CARD COUNTING

If you're counting cards while playing Blackjack, do not increase you bets too much when the deck is rich. Staying within a range of one to three or four units will keep you out of trouble; betting one unit when the deck is poor, three or four when the deck is rich in ten-values.

Several years ago I was asked to leave a Blackjack table. I was varying my bets from $5 to $100 and up depending on the count. In essence, I was shouting to the casino, "Look at me! I am counting cards and winning your money!" Yes, I was stupid. I was winning so much that I became overconfident and slightly cocky. Had I controlled my bets properly, I would've won more money and the casino might have thought I was just lucky.

Even if the casino knows you are counting cards, they will leave you alone so long as your betting range is not outrageous. If it is they will begin to shuffle after every hand, which will put a quick end to your card counting. So if card counting is proving beneficial for you, keep increasing your basic unit or double up after winning hands.

RULE VARIATIONS

Be smart. Use your head. Do not, I repeat *do not* play at casinos where the rules are unfavorable to the player. From reading the rule variations in the earlier chapters, you know that some casinos offer more liberal rules than others. Why gamble at a casino which insists on stacking the odds against you? If all of us stop playing at casinos like those, they will modify their rules to keep our business. So take the time to seek out those casinos which offer the best rules, and give them your business; the effort will mean more money in your pocket.

ALCOHOL

If you are going to let the casino feed you free drinks, exercise restraint. How can you remember proper gambling methods and protect your money if you can't even remember what day it is? Do your drinking while toying with your fun money. If you must drink, keep it in moderation.

COMFORT

In some casinos the gambling tables and machines are so close together that it is impossible to find a comfortable chair. How can you concentrate on gambling when the adjacent player's elbow is constantly banging into your ribs? How can you concentrate when the man behind you keeps pushing his chair into yours? Better yet, how can you concentrate when the lovely lady (or handsome man if you're a lady) next to you has her leg firmly planted against yours? Find a chair with some room around it.

TIME

There aren't any clocks in the casinos, so wear a watch. If your game plan calls for one-hour gambling sessions, you need a way to tell when the hour has passed.

Also, I will be the first to admit that regardless of my time plan, I do not quit when I am winning. I don't care if the plane leaves in ten minutes, I don't quit when things are going my way. Yes, my wife nearly left me in Las Vegas one time because of this attitude, and I've also missed a lot of shows.

INTIMIDATION

Some casino employees (dealers, pit bosses, floorpersons and others) delight in their ability to intimidate people. Do not allow yourself to be intimidated. Don't worry if a pit boss looks at you as though you are doing something wrong, particularly when you are winning, as that may be the way he or she always looks. To some casino employees, every gambler is a potential cheater out to rip off the casino. Do not feel uncomfortable just because you are winning and the floorman is staring at you, peeking over your shoulder, or trying in any manner to distract you. They are simply trying to do their jobs. If you talk to the employees you will find that most of them are very nice, very helpful, real people.

TIPPING (TOKES)

For my money, there is only one time when you should tip (toke) a dealer; when they have worked to make your play as enjoyable as possible. Yes, that means that I tip the good dealers whether I win or lose. Of course, if I'm losing I'm not at the table long enough to decide whether the dealer is a wonderful human being.

I realize that dealing is a difficult job, but some of them are so obnoxious they deserve to be locked in a cage full of gorillas. Some dealers are so discourteous they belong on an island full of lepers. However, there are more good dealers than bad. Tip the good ones and ask the bad ones why they didn't have human parents.

Most dealers prefer that you make a bet for them as your tip. That way a winning hand or roll of the dice can double their tip. I do this at times, but not very often. Ordinarily, I wait until the session is over and then tip the dealer.

Whatever you do, remember this: If you find a particularly enjoyable dealer, and if that same dealer is winning four out of every five hands, change tables. Don't stay at a losing table just because the dealer is entertaining.

REST

Most of us can only stay mentally alert when we are well rested. I realize it is difficult to nap or sleep while you're in such exciting environments, but try to get as much rest as you can. In addition, try to refresh your body and mind with physical exercise, whether it be a walk, a game of tennis or golf, or a few laps in the beautiful swimming pools. Take frequent breaks to remove your mind from gambling. Try to do your gambling an hour or two at a time. However, as I have stated previously, if you find yourself in a situation where the composition of the deck or the "run" of the dice, combined with your playing ability, is proving very lucrative, then give yourself a little more time. Why walk away from a table when you're winning? No, I'm not saying that if you're up one unit you should stay at that table. I'm saying that if you're winning, say, thirty to fifty units, you should stay right where you are *so long as you continue to win*. If you start to lose back a portion of your winnings, say as much as five to seven units, or if you're winning but starting to feel exhausted, move on to the hotel's steam room, hot tub, or a warm bed.

PRACTICE

Prior to the start of your next gambling excursion, practice your specialty. One reading of this book is not enough. You *must* practice the game or games you intend to play. You must have *in-depth* knowledge of your specialty. You don't become a winning tennis professional by reading a book on tennis. Likewise, you can't become a winning gambler by reading a book on gambling. You must practice, practice, practice. Start refreshing your memory a few weeks before you depart for Vegas, Reno, Tunica or wherever. An hour or two of practice each day should suffice.

SELF-CONTROL

None of my suggestions mean anything unless you have the discipline required to use them. You must not let emotions dictate your play. You must be able to control yourself. You can do anything you want . . .with your fun money. But when gambling with your serious money, you must control yourself.

I do not mean to imply that you should not have any fun. If you only gamble with your serious money six hours each day, you only need to discipline yourself for six hours each day. For the other eighteen hours of each day you can get drunk, be a clown, be a fool, be a lover, or be a blithering idiot if you want. Have fun with your fun money and exercise control with your serious money. You'll have an enjoyable *and* profitable time.

CASINO ADVANTAGE

Throughout this book I've listed the various casino advantages on the different wagers available to you. Now, to give added meaning to those cold figures, I'll talk real dollars and cents.

Example 1: You are a $5 bettor, playing Roulette. On every spin of the wheel you bet on either red or black. The casino advantage is 5.26%. You play for three days, averaging twelve hours of playing time each day. The Roulette wheel spins approximately forty times each hour. How much money can you expect to lose?

Here is how to figure it out: Forty bets per hour times twelve hours times three days, equals 1,440 total bets. At $5 per wager, you would then bet a total of $7,200! In gambling parlance, this would be termed $7,200 worth of "action". And if we multiply $7,200 by the casino advantage of 5.26%, we find that you could expect to lose $378.72.

Since you expect to lose only $378, does this mean that you could start play with a bankroll (gambling stake) of only, say, $500? Absolutely not! You may very well lose $900 the first day, win back $300 the second day, and then win another $222 the third day.

Example 2: You are still a $5 bettor, but now you are playing craps, betting on the field. The casino advantage is 11.2%. Field bets are one-roll wagers, so you win or lose on every roll of the dice. You play for three days, you stay at the tables for twelve hours each day, making approximately sixty bets per hour.

Sixty bets per hour times twelve hours times three days equals 2,160 total bets. At $5 per bet, you would wager a total of $10,800. And $10,800 multiplied by the casino advantage of 11.2% would mean losses of $1,209.60.

Example 3: You are playing craps again, still a $5 bettor, but this time you are a little smarter. Since you know the casino advantage on Pass Line is only 1.4%, that is your bet. Also, you are now making fewer bets per hour, because if often takes numerous rolls of the dice to determine whether you win or lose. So we'll say you only make thirty bets per hour.

Thirty bets per hour times twelve hours times three days equals 1,080 total bets. At $5 per bet, your total action would be $5,400, which when multiplied times the casino advantage of 1.4% would equal losses of only $75.60.

Of course you could have gotten lucky and actually won money in one of these examples, but the odds are against you. Plus, the worse the odds, the less chance you have of experiencing consistent wins. When the casino advantage is 1.4% you have a much greater chance of winning than when the advantage is 11.2%.

A tough question: In the future, now that you know the odds and the casino's advantages, which of the games will you play with your serious money, and what bets will you make? If your answer is that you want to be like the person in Examples 1 and 2, above, buying this book was a waste of your money. But if your answer is that you want to be like the person in Example 3, there is definite hope for you.

In Example 3 you have plenty of action, gamble for a long time, have plenty of fun, and lose a minimal share of your gambling stake. Also, since the casino advantage in Example 3 is so narrow, you have an excellent chance of experiencing winning sessions.

Be smart! Protect your money.

Chapter 16

Where To Play

The title for this chapter derives from the fact that it is the question I am asked most frequently. People assume that I have gambled at one heck of a lot of different casinos, that I have done some research, and that I can provide for them a list of the best casinos in the United States. And they are correct. At least to a limited degree. While I have not gambled at virtually every casino in America, many have seen my money. Wherever my travels take me, I make it a point to seek out any casinos in that area. However, I have not been in every state which has legalized casino gambling. Therefore, the list I am about to provide covers only the best of those I have actually visited. If your favorite casino is not on my list, do not fret. It could be that I have never been to your favorite gambling spot. In fact, I have heard of a number of places I have yet to see in person; usually small casinos, so to speak, off the beaten path. I hear there are several terrific casinos in Deadwood, South Dakota. But since I have never been to Deadwood, you won't hear about any of them in this book.

What are my criteria? What is it that puts a casino on my "Best" list? It is very simple. From a gambling perspective, the casinos must offer the gaming rules which are the most advantageous for us players.

Let us say you are in Ely, Nevada. Right. What would you be doing there in the first place? But let us assume that one of your life journeys has beamed you there. Next, we will assume that there are two casinos, one across the street from the other. One, which we will arbitrarily call The Golden Turkey, is brand new. The other, which we will call The Gambler's Dream, is quite old. The Golden Turkey is beautiful. The owners obviously spent a lot of time and money ensuring that their establishment would be perceived as warm and attractive. The Gambler's Dream, however, has not been remodeled for the past twenty-one years. At The Gambler's Dream, everything looks and smells old. Both places have courteous, friendly employees. You have decided to play Blackjack. At The Golden Turkey you find sixteen tables. Wonderful. The minimum wager is only a dollar. Maximum of three hundred. All hands are dealt from a shoe. The dealer has the option of whether to hit or stand on a soft seventeen. Pairs may be split, but not re-split. You can only double down on a holding of ten or eleven. The place looks great, the motel portion has two hundred oversized rooms. You can get one for only $19 a night, and they have a large heated outdoor pool, plus a Jacuzzi, plus an exercise room, plus a free continental breakfast. So, since it looks like a good place to stay, you decide to try your luck. Can you expect to find me playing at a table near you? Have you read this book?

Over at Gambler's Dream they only have thirty rooms, no pool, no Jacuzzi, and no free breakfast. There are only three Blackjack tables. The limits run from two dollars to a thousand. All tables are single deck. The dealer must stand on all seventeens, whether soft or hard. Pairs may be split and re-split, plus you can double down after splitting. You can also double down on any first two cards, regardless of their value. The surrender option is available. Given a choice between The Gambler's Dream and The Golden Turkey, can you guess where I will be playing?

If you are on a holiday, and merely want to have some "fun," keep staying and playing at places like The Golden Turkey. So long as you only play for a dollar a hand, you might have a "fun" time no matter how much money you lose. However, if you want to do some serious gambling, keep looking for The Gambler's Dreams that are out there. Play only at those establishments which give you the best chance of A) avoiding serious losses, or B) winning large sums of money.

Let us say that you play at The Golden Turkey, and I play at The Gambler's Dream. We both play and win exactly the same number of hands. Our timing is so good that we both quickly advance to the maximum bet allowed at our respective tables. Well, hooray for both of us. The only difference is that for the same amount of playing time you generate profits of three or four thousand while I generate profits of fifteen or twenty thousand. Actually, your run is so good that you are wishing there was not a cap of three hundred dollars at The Golden Turkey. My run is so good I am elated that I am *not* playing at The Golden Turkey.

What if we were playing craps and got into a really hot game? Would you rather be playing at The Golden Turkey, where they offer only single odds bets, or over at The Gambler's Dream, where you can take up to ten times odds?

I believe I have made my point. There are, for example, some great architectural wonders in Las Vegas; places which have outstanding rooms and facilities, motifs and decor. In other words, establishments which are wonderful resorts for tourists. And if all you want to do is "vacation," you should stay at those places. Stay there, but do not gamble there. Help all of us gamblers by staying and playing at hotel/casinos which offer the best gambling rules. If a hotel/casino finds out they can do a fabulous business even though their rules are ridiculous, they will never change their rules. Why should they?

Okay, here they are. At the time of this writing, all of these places had the rules we want. In addition, most of them also have all the other elements we would like to see such as courteous employees, good food and drink, and an atmosphere conducive to serious gambling:

1. *Binion's Horseshoe Club Hotel and Casino*, Downtown Las Vegas

2. *Four Queens Hotel and Casino*, Downtown Las Vegas

3. *Golden Nugget Hotel and Casino*, Downtown Las Vegas

4. *Sam Boyd's Fremont Hotel and Casino*, Downtown Las Vegas

5. *Golden Gate Hotel and Casino*, Downtown Las Vegas

6. *Barbary Coast Hotel and Casino*, Las Vegas Strip

7. *Sam's Town Hotel and Casino* Robinsonville, Miss. & Offstrip Las Vegas

8. *Buffalo Bill's Hotel and Casino*, Jean, Nevada

9. *Boomtown Hotel and Casino*
Off-strip Las Vegas

10. *Palace Station Hotel and Casino*, Off-strip Las Vegas

11. *Colorado Belle Hotel and Casino*, Laughlin, Nevada

12. *Ramada Express Hotel and Casino*, Laughlin, Nevada

13. *Silver Smith Casino Resort* Wendover, Nevada

14. *Stateline Casino*, Wendover, Nevada

15. *Hollywood Hotel and Casino* Robinsonville, Mississippi

16. *Si Reed's Peppermill Oasis* Mesquite, Nevada

17. *Slots-A-Fun Casino*, Las Vegas Strip

18. *Silver City Casino*, Las Vegas Strip

19. *Stardust Hotel and Casino*, Las Vegas Strip

20. *Riviera Hotel and Casino*, Las Vegas Strip

"What?," you scream. How about Caesar's in Atlantic City? Or, how could I possibly leave out Circus Circus? Is this guy an advertisement for Las Vegas? Hasn't he ever heard of the Menominee Nation Casino in Wisconsin? Why isn't Harrah's in Shreveport on this list?

Good questions, all. The answers? At Caesar's in Atlantic City there are no single or double deck blackjack games, and the minimums are too high. At Circus Circus there are just too darn many kids running around. Las Vegas just happens to be the place with the most casinos in the world, so it is only natural that they would have more names on my list than any other place. No, I have never heard of the place in Wisconsin. And the reason Harrah's Shreveport is not on the list is that I have never been there. But if they are like all the other Harrah's Casinos, it is probably a great place but does not offer the best rules.

Note that my top five are all in downtown Vegas. All five are great places to gamble, *plus* they are all within easy walking distance of one another. Remember earlier in this book when I mentioned that if you were not enjoying any success you should move to another table, or another casino? Well, how much more can you ask for then to have five great ones darn near bordering each other? Afraid to go downtown because you have heard the area is populated with bums and drifters?

Then you have not been to the "new" downtown. (Truth be told, I liked the "old" downtown, too.)

Another question. How did I come up with these off-strip casinos which you may never have heard of before? Very simple. I asked the locals where they liked to play, and then went there. For you see, the people who both live and gamble in Las Vegas have a tremendous choice of places to wager their money. Consequently, they can be very selective. Which is why you will not find very many locals playing at the the strip resort destinations.

Do I sound as if I do not like the strip? Well, as you can see from my list, there are several spots on the strip that I recommend. Four of them, numbers 17 through 20, are located so that a ten minute walk will carry you past each of them, and that be good.

But why, you still ask, is your list so heavily oriented towards Nevada, particularly southern Nevada? Have I ever been to Reno or Lake Tahoe? Of course I have. And there are some very nice casinos in both locations. But most of them only allow a blackjack double down on 10 or 11, and on a list which is this competitive, that is enough to disqualify them from consideration. And while I have not been to every casino in every state, I have played on several of the riverboats in Illinois. Yes, I have been to Indian Reservation casinos in California. Yes, I have played in Colorado. And Nevada, whether you are in Laughlin, Jean, Wendover or Vegas, has more places with better rules than any place I have ever seen. Hopefully the business in other states will become so competitive that the casinos will all start to offer the best rules and games. Until they do, they cannot make my list.

I will say it one last time. If you are going to gamble strictly for fun, you can do it most anywhere. However, if you are intent on actually winning, then you must gamble at those casinos which offer you the best possibilities for achieving your goals.

GOOD LUCK!

RECOMMENDED READING

Here are several suggestions for those of you who want to dig a little deeper.

1. For blackjack, make a trip down to your local library and see if they have either of these two books: *Scarne on Cards*, by John Scarne, or *Beat the Dealer*, by Edward Thorp. Scarne's book is out of print. Thorp's book is still available. Both are a must for any serious gambler.

2. For craps, seek out and purchase *John Patrick's Craps*. It could become your craps bible.

3. For more on blackjack, or craps, plus all the other games of chance, obtain the free catalog offered by Gambler's Book Shop. Their address is 630 South 11th Street, Las Vegas, Nevada, 89101. As this goes to press, they also have a toll-free number, 800-522-1777 or fax, 1-702-382-7594. Via Internet, http:// www.gamblersbook.com. They offer a huge selection of books on all aspects of casino gambling, plus computer software and video tapes.

CASINOS OF
NORTH AMERICA

So, your wife (or husband) wants to visit a distant relative who lives in, of all places, Tokio, North Dakota. One of the garden spots of America, but certainly no place you are eager to visit. You would rather spend the same time in the casino of your choice. Well, guess what? There is a way for both of you to be happy. Your better half can visit the relative while you gamble, because, believe it or not, there is a small casino in Tokio, North Dakota.

In fact, there are small and large casinos spread out all over North America. Many in places you never heard of, many in places which may surprise you. Not all of them are first-class Vegas-type casinos which offer all the gambling venues we would like to see, some of them are nothing more than a handful of slot machines. But the growth of casinos is spreading across the continent faster than you can borrow money on your credit card. The total number of casinos in North America is staggering, especially to those of us who think only in terms of Nevada and New Jersey. So, in the interest of maximizing your education, I am herewith providing a listing of every, at the time of this writing, casino in North America. I am certain that by the time this gets into print many others will have been born. If I missed any, I apologize.

Even if you have no interest in knowing whether there are any casinos in Missouri, take a few minutes some time to browse through this list. If nothing else, you will be entertained by the creative names of some of these places.

Arizona

Apache Gold Casino
San Carlos, Arizona 85550
800-272-2433

Bucky's Casino
At Prescott Resort Center
Prescott, Arizona 86301
800-756-8744

Casino of the Sun
7406 S. Camino De Oeste Road
Tucson, Arizona 85746
800-344-9435

Cliff Castle Casino
353 Middle Verde Road
Camp Verde, Arizona 86322
520-567-9031

Cocopah Bingo and Casino
Somerton, Arizona 85350
800-237-5687

Desert Diamond Casino
7350 S. Old Nogales Hwy
Tucson, Arizona 85734
602-294-7777

Fort McDowell Casino
Fountain Hills, Arizona 85269
800-843-3678

Gila River Casino
5512 Wild Horse Path
Chandler, Arizona 85226
800-946-4452

Gila River Casino
1201 South 56th Street
Chandler, Arizona 85226
800-946-4452

Harrah's Phoenix Ak-Chin Casino
Maricopa, Arizona 85239
800-427-7247

Hon-Dah Casino
Pinetop, Arizona 85935
602-369-0299

Hualapi Casino
Meadview, Arizona 86444
520-699-4161

Mazatzal Casino
Payson, Arizona 85547
880-552-0938

Pipe Springs Resort & Casino
Fredonia, Arizona 86022
801-559-6537

Yavapai Gaming Center
Prescott, Arizona 86301
520-445-6219

California

Barona Casino
1000 Wildcat Canyon Road
Lakeside, California 92040
800-227-8238

Bicycle Club Casino
7301 Eastern Avenue
Bell Gardens, California 90201
800-292-0015

Cache Creek Indian Bingo & Casino
14455 Highway 16
Brooks, California 95606
916-796-3118

Casino Morongo
Cabazon, California 92230
800-775-4386

Cher-Ae Heights Bingo
Trinidad, California 95570
707-677-3611

Chicken Ranch Bingo
16929 Chicken Ranch Road
Jamestown, California 95327
800-762-4646

Colusa Bingo & Casino
3770 Highway 45
Colusa, California 95932
800-655-8946

Commerce Casino
6131 E. Telegraph Road
Commerce, California 90040
800-287-7758

El Dorado
15411 S. Vermont Avenue
Gardena, California 90247
310-323-2800

Fantasy Springs Casino
84-245 Indio Springs Drive
Indio, California 92203
619-342-5000

Hi-Desert Casino
11711 Air Base sRoad
Adelanto, California 92301
619-246-8624

Hollywood Park Casino
1088 S. Prairie Avenue
Hollywood, California 90301
310-330-2800

Jackson Indian Bingo & Casino
12222 New York Ranch Road
Jackson, California 95642
209-223-1677

Normandie Casino & Showroom
1045 W. Rosenthans Avenue
Gardena, California 90427
310-352-3400

Palace Bingo
17225 Jersey Avenue
Leemoore, California 93245
209-924-7751

Robinson Rancheria Bingo & Casino
1545 E. Highway 20
Nice, California 95464
800-809-3636

San Manuel Indian Bingo & Casino
5797 N. Victoria Avenue
Highland, California 92346
800-359-2464

Spotlight 29 Casino
46-200 Harrison Street
Coachella, California 92236
619-775-5566

Sycuan Gaming Center
5469 Dehesa Road
El Cajon, California 92019
800-278-2826

Table Mountain Rancheria
Casino & Bingo
8184 Friant Road
Friant, California 93626
800-541-3637

Viejas Valley Casino
5000 Willows Road
Alpine, California 91901
800-847-6537

Win-River Casino & Bingo
2100 Rancheria Road
Redding, California 96001
800-280-8946

Colorado

Aspen Mine & Casino
166 E. Bennett Avenue
Cripple Creek, Colorado 80813
719-689-0770

Baby Doe's Silver Dollar Casino
102A Lawrence Street
Central City, Colorado 80427
303-582-5510

Best Western's Gold Rush
Hotel & Casino
425 E. Bennett Avenue
Cripple Creek, Colorado 80813
800-235-8239

Black Diamond Casino
425 E. Bennett Avenue
Cripple Creek, Colorado 80813
719-689-2898

Black Hawk Station
141 Gregory Street
Black Hawk, Colorado 80422
303-582-5582

Blazing Saddles Casino
139 Main Street
Black Hawk, Colorado 80422
303-582-0707

Bronco Billy's Sports Bar & Casino
233 E. Bennett Avenue
Cripple Creek, Colorado 80813
719-689-2142

Bronco Billy's Sports Bar & Casino
125 Gregory Street
Black Hawk, Colorado 80422
800-298-7424

Bull Durham Saloon & Casino
110 Main Street
Black Hawk, Colorado 80422
303-582-0810

Bullwhackers Casino
101 Gregory Street
Black Hawk, Colorado 80422
303-271-2500

Bullwhackers Casino
130 Main Street
Central City, Colorado 80427
800-426-2855

Central Palace Casino
132 Lawrence Street
Central City, Colorado 80427
800-822-7466

Colorado Central Station Casino
340 Main Street
Black Hawk, Colorado 80422
303-582-3000

Colorado Grand Gaming Parlour
300 E. Bennett Avenue
Cripple Creek, Colorado 80813
719-689-3517

Crooks Palace
200 Gregory Street
Black Hawk, Colorado 80422
303-582-0810

Doc Holiday Casino
101 Main Street
Central City, Colorado 80427
303-582-1400

Dostal Alley Saloon &
Gambling Emporium
1 Dostal Alley
Central City, Colorado 80427
303-582-1610

Eureka Casino
211 Gregory Street
Black Hawk, Colorado 80422
303-582-1040

Gilpin Hotel Casino
119 Main Street
Black Hawk, Colorado 80422
303-582-1133

Gold Mine Casino
130 Clear Creek
Black Hawk, Colorado 80422
303-582-0711

Gold Rush Hotel & Casino
209 Bennett
Cripple Creek, Colorado 80813
800-235-8239

Golden Gates Casino
261 Main Street
Black Hawk, Colorado 80422
303-277-1650

Golden Rose Casino
102 Main Street
Central City, Colorado 80427
303-582-5060

Harrah's Casino
131 Main Street
Black Hawk, Colorado 80422
303-777-1111

Harrah's Casino
131 Main Street
Central City, Colorado 80427
303-562-1171

Harvey's Wagon Wheel Hotel & Casino
321 Gregory Street
Central City, Colorado 80427
303-582-0800

Imperial Hotel & Casino
123 N. 3rd Street
Cripple Creek, Colorado 80813
719-689-7777

Independence Hotel & Casino
151 E. Bennett Avenue
Cripple Creek, Colorado 80813
719-689-2925

Jazz Alley Casino
321 Main Street
Black Hawk, Colorado 80422
303-426-1337

Johnny Nolan's Saloon &
Gambling Emporium
301 E. Bennett Avenue
Cripple Creek, Colorado 80813
719-689-3598

The Jubilee Casino
351 Myers Avenue
Cripple Creek, Colorado 80813
719-689-2519

Lady Luck Casino
120 Main Street
Central City, Colorado 80427
303-582-1603

Legends Casino
200 Bennett Street
Cripple Creek, Colorado 80813
800-528-6533

Long Branch Saloon & Casino
200 E. Bennett Avenue
Cripple Creek, Colorado 80813
800-528-6533

Lucky Lola's Casino
251 E. Bennett Avenue
Cripple Creek, Colorado 80813
719-689-3140

Lucky Star Casino
221 Gregory Street
Black Hawk, Colorado 80422
303-582-1122

Maverick's Casino & Steakhouse
411 E. Bennett Avenue
Cripple Creek, Colorado 80813
719-689-2737

Midnight Rose Hotel & Casino
256 E. Bennett Avenue
Cripple Creek, Colorado 80813
719-689-0303

Narrow Guage Gaming Depot
418 E. Bennett Avenue
Cripple Creek, Colordo 80813
719-689-3214

Old Chicago Casino
419 E. Bennett Avenue
Cripple Creek, Colorado 80813
719-689-7880

Otto's Casino/Black Forest Inn
260 Gregory Street
Black Hawk, Colorado 80422
303-582-0150

Palace Hotel & Casino
712 E. Bennett Avenue
Cripple Creek, Colorado 80813
719-689-2992

Papone's Palace Casino
118 Main Street
Central City, Colorado 80427
303-279-9291

Phenix House Gaming/Bed & Breakfast
232 E. Bennett Avenue
Cripple Creek, Colorado 80813
719-689-2030

Red Dolly Casino
530 Gregory Street
Black Hawk, Colorado 80422
303-582-1100

Rohling Inn Casino
160 Gregory Street
Black Hawk, Colorado 80422
303-582-9343

Silver Palace Casino
404 E. Bennett Avenue
Cripple Creek, Colorado 80813
719-689-3980

Sky Ute Lodge & Casino
Hwy. 172 N
Ignacio, Colorado 81137
800-876-7017

Star of Cripple Creek
143 E. Bennett Avenue
Cripple Creek, Colorado 80813
719-689-7827

Teller House Casino
120 Eureka Street
Central City, Colorado 80427
800-773-7568

Ute Mountain Casino
3 Weeminuche Drive
Towaoc, Colorado 81334
800-258-8007

Virgin Mule Casino
269 E. Bennett Avenue
Cripple Creek, Colorado 80813
719-689-2734

Wild Bill's Pub/Gaming Parlor/Hotel
220 E. Bennett Avenue
Cripple Creek, Colorado 80813
719-689-2707

Wild Wild West Brewpub & Casino
443 E. Bennett Avenue
Cripple Creek, Colorado 80813
719-689-3736

Womack's Saloon & Gaming Parlor
210 E. Bennett Avenue
Cripple Creek, Colorado 80813
719-689-0333

Connecticut

Foxwoods Resort Casino
Route 2
Ledyard, Connecticut 06339
800-752-9244

Illinois

Alton Belle Riverboat Casino
219 Piasa Street
Alton, Illinois 62002
800-336-7568

Casino Queen
200 S. Front Street
East St. Louis, Illinois 62201
800-777-0777

Empress Casino
2300 Empress Drive
Joliet, Illinois 60434
708-345-6789

The Grand Victorian Casino
250 S. Grove Avenue
Elgin, Illinois 60120
708-888-1000

Harrah's Joliet Casino
Northern Star/Southern Star Riverboats
150 N. Scott Street
Joliet, Illinois 60431
800-427-7247

Hollywood Casino
City of Lights 1 & 11 Riverboats
1 New York Street Bridge
Aurora, Illinois 60506
800-888-7777

Jumer's Casino
18th Street at Mississippi River
Rock Island, Illinois 61204
800-477-7747

Par-A-Dice Riverboat Casino
21 Blackjack Boulevard
East Peoria, Illinois 61611
309-698-7711

Player's Casino
207 S. Ferry Street
Metropolis, Illinois 62960
800-929-5905

Silver Eagle Casino
19731 RR 20 W
East Dubuque, Illinois 61025
815-747-2455

Iowa
Belle of Sioux City Casino
100 Chris Larsen Park
Sioux City, Iowa 51102
800-424-0080

Bluffs Run Casino
2701 23rd Avenue
Council Bluffs, Iowa 51501
800-238-2946

Casino Omaha
1 Blackford Bend Boulevard
Onawa, Iowa 51040
800-858-8238

Catfish Bend Riverboat
North Front Street
Fort Madison, Iowa 52601
319-372-2946

Dubuque Diamond Jo
3rd Street Ice Harbor
Dubuque, Iowa 52004
319-583-7005

Lady Luck Casino
1777 15th Street
Bettendorf, Iowa 52722
800-724-5825

Meskwaki Casino
1504 305th Street
Tama, Iowa 52339
800-728-4263

Miss Marquette Riverboat
Casino & Resort
99 Anti/Monopoly
Marquette, Iowa 52158
800-496-8238

Mississippi Belle ll Riverboat Casino
311 Riverview Drive
Clinton, Iowa 52732
800-457-9975

Prarie Meadows Race Track & Casino
1 Prarie Meadows Drive
Altoona, Iowa 50009
800-325-9015

The President Riverboat
130 W. River Drive
Davenport, Iowa 52801
800-262-8711

Winna Vegas Casino
1500 330 St.
Sloan, Iowa 51055
800-468-9466

Louisiana
Belle of Baton Rouge
103 France Street
Baton Rouge, Louisiana 70802
504-378-6000

Belle of Orleans
Bally's Casino Lakeside Resort
1 Stars and Stripes Boulevard
New Orleans, Louisiana 70126
800-572-2559

Boomtown Casino
4132 Peters Road
Harvey, Louisiana 70059
800-366-7711

Casino Rouge
1717 River Road N
Baton Rouge, Louisiana 70802
504-381-7777

Cypress Bayou Casino
832 Martin Luther King Road
Charenton, Louisiana 70523
800-284-4386

Flamingo Casino
Poydras St. Wharf
New Orleans, Louisiana 70130
800-587-5825

Grand Casino Avoyelles
711 E. Tunica Drive
Marksville, Louisiana 71351
318-253-1946

Grand Casino Coushatta
777 Coushatta Drive
Kinder, Louisiana 70648
800-584-7263

Harrah's Casino
365 Canal Street
New Orleans, Louisiana 70130
504-533-6000

Harrah's Casino
315 Clyde Fant Parkway
Shreveport, Louisiana 71101
318-424-7777

Horseshoe Casino & Hotel
711 Horseshoe Boulevard
Bossier City, Louisiana 71111
800-895-0711

Isle of Capri Casino
711 Ise of Capri Boulevard
Bossier, Louisiana 71111
318-678-7777

Player's Casino
507 North Lakeshore Drive
Lake Charles, Louisiana 70601
800-977-7529

River City Casino
Grand Palais & Crescent City Riverboats
1400 Annunciation
New Orleans, Louisiana 70130
800-600-6880

Star Casino
507 North Lakeshore Drive
Lake Charles, Louisiana 70601
318-433-0541

Treasure Chest Casino
5050 Williams Boulevard
Kenner, Louisiana 70065
800-298-0711

Michigan

Chip-In Motel & Casino
& Hannahville Bingo
Highway 2 & Highway 41
Harris, Michigan 49845
800-682-6040

Kewadin Shores Casino
3039 Mackinac Trail
St. Ignace, Michigan 49781
906-643-7071

Kewadin Slots
102 Candy Cane Lane
Christmas, Michigan 49862
906-387-5475

Kewadin Slots
Manistique, Michigan 49854
906-341-5510

Kewadin Slots
Three Mile Road
Hessel, Michigan 49745
906-484-2903

Kings Club Casino/
Bay Mills Indian Comm. Bingo
Lakeshore Drive
Brimley, Michigan 49715
906-248-3241

Lac Vieux Desert Casino
Choate Road
Watersmeet, Michigan 49969
906-358-4226

Leelanau Sands Casino
2521 NW Bayshore Drive
Suttons Bay, Michigan 49682
800-922-2946

Leelanau Super Gaming Palace
2521 NW Bayshore Drive
Suttons Bay, Michigan 49682
616-271-6852

Ojibwa Casino Resort
Highway 38
Baraga, Michigan 49908
800-323-8045

Soaring Eagle Casino
2395 S. Leaton Road
Mt. Pleasant, Michigan 48858
517-722-8900

Vegas Kewadin Casino
2186 Skunk road
Sault Ste.Marie, Michigan 49783
800-539-2346

Minnesota

Black Bear Casino
601 Highway 210
Carlton, Minnesota 55718
218-878-2327

Firefly Creek Casino
Rural Route 2
Granite Falls, Minnesota 56241
612-564-2121

Fond-du-Luth Casino
129 E. Superior Street
Duluth, Minnesota 55802
800-873-0280

Fortune Bay Casino
1430 Boise Forte Road
Tower, Minnesota 55790
800-992-7529

Grand Casino
777 Lady Luck Drive
Hinckley, Minnesota 55037
800-472-6321

Grand Casino
777 Grand Avenue
Onamia, Minnesota 56359
800-626-5825

Grand Portage Lodge & Casino
Marina Road
Grand Portage, Minnesota 55605
800-543-1384

Jackpot Junction Casino
Highway 212 & U.S. 71
Morton, Minnesota 56270
507-644-7800

Lake of the Woods Lodge & Casino
1012 E. Lake Street
Warroad, Minnesota 56763
800-568-6649

Mystic Lake Casino &
Dakota Country Casino
2400 Mystic Lake Boulevard
Prior Lake, Minnesota 55372
800-262-7799

Northern Lights Casino
Highway 371 & Highway 200
Walker, Minnesota 56484
800-252-7529

Palace Bingo & Casino
Bingo Palace Drive
Cass Lake, Minnesota 56633
800-228-6676

Red Lake Casino & Bingo
Thief River Falls, Minnesota 56701
800-568-6649

River Road Casino
Highway 3 & Highway 59
Thief River Falls, Minnesota 56701
218-681-4062

Shooting Star Casino
777 Casino Road
Mahnomen, Minnesota 56557
800-453-7827

Treasure Island Casino & Bingo
5734 Sturgeon Lake Road
Welch, Minnesota 55089
800-222-7077

Mississippi

Ameristar Casino
4146 S. Washington Street
Vicksburg, Mississippi 39180
800-700-7770

Bally's Saloon/Gambling Hall/Hotel
1450 Bally Boulevard
Tunica, Mississippi 38676
800-382-2559

Bayou Caddy's Jubilee Casino
222 S. Theobald
Greenville, Mississippi 38702
800-552-0707

Bayou Caddy's Jubilee Casino
5005 S. Beach Boulevard
Lakeshore, Mississippi 39558
601-436-7777

Boomtown Casino
676 Bayview Avenue
Biloxi, Mississippi 89439
800-627-0777

Casino Magic
711 Casino Magic Drive
Bay St. Louis, Mississippi 39520
800-562-4425

Casino Magic
195 E. Beach Boulevard
Biloxi, Mississippi 39530
800-562-4425

Circus Belle Casino
1010 Casino Center Drive
Robinsonville, Mississippi 38664
601-357-1111

Copa Casino
777 Copa Boulevard
Gulfport, Mississippi 39502
601-863-3330

Cotton Club Casino
Greenville, Mississippi 38702
800-946-6673

Fitzgerald's Casino
711 Lucky Lane
Robinsonville, Mississippi 38664
800-766-5825

Grand Casino
265 Beach Boulevard
Biloxi, Mississippi 39530
800-946-2946

Grand Casino
3215 W. Beach Boulevard
Gulfport, Mississippi 39501
800-946-7777

Harrah's Casino
1310 Mulberry Street
Vicksburg, Mississippi 39180
601-636-3423

Harrah's Casino
711 Harrah's Drive
Robinsonville, Mississippi 38664
800-427-7247

Hollywood Casino
Commerce Landing
Robinsonville, Mississippi 38664
800-871-0711

Isle of Capri Casino &
Crown Plaza Resort
151 Beach Boulevard
Biloxi, Mississippi 39530
601-435-5400

Isle of Capri Casino
3990 Washington Street
Vicksburg, Mississippi 39180
800-946-4753

Lady Luck Casino
1848 Beach Boulevard
Biloxi, Mississippi 39531
800-539-5825

Lady Luck Casino
21 Silver Street
Natchez, Mississippi 39121
800-722-5825

Lady Luck Rhythm & Blues Casino Hotel
777 Lady Luck Parkway
Lula, Mississippi 38644
800-789-5825

Las Vegas Casino
242 Walnut Street
Greenville, Mississippi 38701
800-834-2721

Palace Casino
182 E. Howard Avenue
Biloxi, Mississippi 39533
601-432-8888

President Casino
2110 Beach Boulevard
Biloxi, Mississippi 39533
800-843-7737

Rainbow Casino
1380 Warrenton Road
Vicksburg, Misissippi 39180
800-503-3777

Sam's Town Hotel & Gambling Hall
1477 Casino Strip Boulevard
Robinsonville, Mississippi 38664
800-456-0711

Sheraton Casino
1107 Casino Center Drive
Robinsonville, Mississippi 38664
800-391-3777

Silver Star Hotel & Casino
Highway 16 West
Philadelphia, Mississippi 39350
800-557-0711

Treasure Bay Casino
One Treasure Bay Drive
Robinsonville, Mississippi 38664
800-727-7684

Treasure Bay Casino Resort
1980 Beach Boulevard
Biloxi, Mississippi 39531
602-385-6000

Missouri

Argosy Casino
I-635N & Highway 9
Riverside, Missouri 64150
800-900-3423

Casino Aztar
Caruthersville, Missouri 63830
314-333-1000

Harrah's Casino
One Riverboat Drive
North Kansas City, Missouri 64116
800-427-7247

President Casino
Admiral Riverboat
Lenor Kay Sullivan Boulevard
St. Louis, Missouri 63102
314-622-1111

St. Charles Riverfront Station
1355 5th Street
St. Charles, Missouri 63302
800-325-7777

St. Jo Frontier Casino
77 Francis Street
St. Joseph, Missouri 64501
800-888-2946

Nevada

Aladdin Hotel & Casino
3667 S. Las Vegas Boulevard
Las Vegas, Nevada 89193
800-634-3428

Alpine Lodge & Nevada Club Casino
Highway 50
Eureka, Nevada 89316
702-237-5365

Arizona Charlie's Inc.
740 S. Decatur Boulevard
Las Vegas, Nevada 89107
800-342-2695

Aztec Inn Casino
2200 S. Las V egas Boulevard
Las Vegas, Nevada 89104
702-385-4566

Baldini's Sports Casino
865 S. Rock Boulevard
Sparks, Nevada 89431
800-845-7911

Bally's Casino
3645 S. Las Vegas Boulevard
Las Vegas, Nevada 89109
800-634-3434

Barbary Coast Hotel & Casino
3595 S. Las Vegas Boulevard
Las Vegas, Nevada 89109
800-634-6755

Barcelona Hotel & Casino
5011 E. Craig Road
Las Vegas, Nevada 89115
800-223-6330

Barton's Club 93
Highway 93
Jackpot, Nevada 89825
800-258-2937

Beano's Casino
7200 W. Lake Mead Boulevard
Las Vegas, Nevada 89128
702-255-9150

Best Western Bonanza Inn & Casino
855 W. Williams Avenue
Fallon, Nevada 89407
702-423-6031

Best Western Main Street
1000 N. Main
Las Vegas, Nevada 89101
702-382-3455

Best Western Mardi Gras Inn
3500 Paradise Road
Las Vegas, Nevada 89109
800-634-6501

Big Dog's Bar & Grill
1511 N. Nellis Boulevard
Las Vegas, Nevada 89110
702-459-1099

Big Dog's Cafe & Casino
6390 W. Sahara Avenue
Las Vegas, Nevada 89102
702-876-3647

Big Game Club
4747 Faircenter Park
Las Vegas, Nevada 89102
702-870-0087

Bill Ladd's Silver Dollar Saloon
2501 E. Charleston Boulevard
Las Vegas, Nevada 89104
702-382-6921

Bill's Casino/Lake Tahoe Harrahs
Highway 50 at State Line
Stateline, Nevada 89449
702-588-2455

Binion's Horseshoe Club Hotel & Casino
128 Fremont Street
Las Vegas, Nevada 89109
800-937-6537

Boardwalk Hotel & Casino
3750 S. Las Vegas Boulevard
Las Vegas, Nevada 89109
800-635-4581

Bob Cashell's Horseshoe
Club & Casino
229 N. Virginia Street
Reno, Nevada 89502
800-962-8413

Bonanza Casino
4720 N. Virginia Street
Reno, Nevada 89503
702-323-2724

Bonanza Lounge
4300 E. Bonanza Road
Las Vegas, Nevada 89110

Bonanza Saloon
Virginia City, Nevada 89440
702-847-0655

Boomtown
3333 Blue Diamond Road
Las Vegas, Nevada 89139
800-263-7777

Border Inn
Highway 50
Baker, Nevada 89311
702-234-7300

Bordertown
19575 Highway 395N
Reno, Nevada 89506
800-443-4383

Boulder Station Hotel & Casino
4111 Boulder Highway
Las Vegas, Nevada 89121
800-544-2411

Bourbon Street Hotel & Casino
120 E. Flamingo Road
Las Vegas, Nevada 89109
800-634-6956

Bruno's Country Club Casino
445 Main Street
Gevlach, Nevada 89412
702-557-2220

Bucket of Blood Saloon
1 South C Street
Virginia City, Nevada 89440
702-847-0322

Buffalo Bill's Resort & Casino
I-15 at State Line
Jean, Nevada 89019
800-367-7383

Burro Inn
Route 95
Beatty, Nevada 89003
702-553-2445

Cactus Jack's Senator Club Casino
420 N. Carson Street
Carson City, Nevada 89701
702-882-8770

Cactus Pete's Resort Casino
Highway 93
Jackpot, Nevada 89825
800-442-3833

Caesars Palace
3570 S. Las Vegas Boulevard
Las Vegas, Nevada 89109
800-634-6661

Caesars Tahoe Resort
Stateline, Nevada 89449
800-648-3353

Cal-Nev-Ari Casino Corporation
1 Paiute Valley Drive
Cal-Nev-Ari, Nevada 89039
702-297-1118

Cal-Nev-Ari Casino & Blue Sky Motel
1 Spirit Mountain
Cal-Nev-Ari, Nevada 89309
702-297-1118

Cal-Neva Lodge & Casino
Crystal Bay, Nevada 89402
800-225-6382

Cal's Jackpot Casino
3012 Griswold Street
North Las Vegas, Nevada 89030
702-399-2269

Captain's Quarters
2610 Regatta Drive
Las Vegas, Nevada 89128
702-256-6200

Carson Horseshoe
402 N. Carson Street
Carson City, Nevada 89701
702-883-2211

Carson Nugget Casino
507 N. Carson Street
Carson City, Nevada 89701
800-426-5239

Carson Station Hotel & Casino
Carson City, Nevada 89701
702-883-0900

Carson Valley Inn Hotel & Casino
1627 Highway 395
Minden, Nevada 89423
800-321-6983

Casino Royale & Hotel
3411 S. Las Vegas Boulevard
Las Vegas, Nevada 89109
702-737-3500

Casino West
11 N. Main Street
Yerington, Nevada 89447
800-227-4661

Castaways Casino
3132 S. Highland Drive
Las Vegas, Nevada 89109
800-552-6363

Charlie's Lakeside Bar & Grill
8603 W. Sahara Avenue
Las Vegas, Nevada 89117
702-258-5170

Cheers Hotel & Casino
567 W. 4th Street
Reno, Nevada 89503
702-322-8181

Circus Circus Hotel & Casino
2880 S. Las Vegas Boulevard
Las Vegas, Nevada 89114
800-444-2472

Circus Circus Hotel & Casino
500 N. Sierra Street
Reno, Nevada 89513
800-648-5010

Clarion Hotel Casino
3800 S. Virginia Street
Reno, Nevada 89502
800-723-6500

Club Cal-Neva Casino
Carson City Satellite
38 E. 2nd Street
Reno, Nevada 89505
800-723-6500

Coin Castle
15 E. Fremont Street
Las Vegas, Nevada 89101
702-385-7474

Colonial Inn Hotel & Casino
250 N. Arlington Avenue
Reno, Nevada 89501
800-336-7366

Colorado Belle Hotel & Casino
2100 S. Casino Drive
Laughlin, Nevada 89028
800-458-9500

Colt Service Center & Casino
650 W. Front Street
Battle Mountain, Nevada 89820
702-635-5424

Commercial Hotel & Casino
345 4th Street
Elko, Nevada 89801
702-738-3181

Comstock Hotel & Casino
200 W. 2nd Street
Reno, Nevada 89501
800-824-8167

Continental Hotel & Casino
4100 Paradise Road
Las Vegas, Nevada 89109
800-777-4844

Copper Queen Hotel & Casino
701 Avenue 1
Ely, Nevada 89301
800-851-9526

Country Club
Gerlach, Nevada 89412
702-557-2220

Crystal Bay Club Casino
Highway 28
Crystal Bay, Nevada 89402
702-831-0512

Dan's Royal Flush Casino
3049 S. Las Vegas Boulevard
Las Vegas, Nevada 89109
800-896-0777

Danny's Slot Country
4213 Boulder Highway
Las Vegas, Nevada 89121
702-451-4974

Days Inn/Town Hall Casino
4155 Koval Lane
Las Vegas, Nevada 89109
702-731-2111

Debbie Reynolds Hotel, Casino,
& Hollywood Movie Museum
305 Convention Center Drive
Las Vegas, Nevada 89109
800-633-1777

Delta Saloon
18 South C Street
Virginia City, Nevada 89440
702-827-0789

Depot Casino & Restaurant
875 W. Williams Avenue
Fallon, Nevada 89406
702-423-2411

Desert Inn Hotel
3145 S. Las Vegas Boulevard
Las Vegas, Nevada 89109
800-634-6909

Don Laughin's Riverside Resort
Hotel & Casino
1650 Casino Drive
Laughlin, Nevada 89029
800-227-3849

Draft House Bar & Casino
4543 N. Rancho Drive
Las Vegas, Nevada 89130
702-645-1404

Ed's Tahoe Nugget
Stateline, Nevada 89449
702-588-7733

Eddie's Fabulous 50's
45 W. 2nd Street
Reno, Nevada 89501
702-329-1950

Edgewater Hotel & Casino
2020 S. Casino Drive
Laughlin, Nevada 89028
800-677-4837

El Capitan Lodge & Casino
540 F Street
Hawthorne, Nevada 89415
702-945-3322

El Cortex Hotel & Casino
600 E. Fremont
Las Vegas, Nevada 89101
800-634-6703

Eldorado Casino
140 S. Water Street
Henderson, Nevada 89015
702-564-1811

Eldorado Hotel Casino
345 N. Virginia Street
Reno, Nevada 89505
800-648-5966

Ellis Island Casino
4178 Koval Lane
Las Vegas, Nevada 89109
702-733-8901

Ernie's Casino
1901 N. Rancho Drive
Las Vegas, Nevada 89106
702-646-4855

Eureka Casino
595 E. Sahara Avenue
Las Vegas, Nevada 89104
702-794-3464

Excalibur Hotel & Casino
3850 S. Las Vegas Boulevard
Las Vegas, Nevada 89119
800-937-7777

Exchange Club of Beatty
604 Main Street
Beatty, Nevada 89003
702-553-2368

Fallon Nugget
70 S. Main Street
Fallon, Nevada 89407
702-423-3111

Fiesta Hotel & Casino
333 N. Rancho Drive
North Las Vegas, Nevada 89106
702-631-7000

Fitzgeralds Casino Hotel
301 Fremont Street
Las Vegas, Nevada 89101
800-274-5825

Fitzgeralds Casino & Hotel
255 N. Virginia Street
Reno, Nevada 89501
800-648-5022

Flamingo Hilton Hotel & Casino
3555 S. Las Vegas Boulevard
Las Vegas, Nevada 89109
800-732-2111

Flamingo Hilton Hotel & Casino
1900 S. Casino Drive
Laughlin, Nevada 89029
800-352-6464

Flamingo Hilton Hotel & Casino
255 North Sierra Street
Reno, Nevada 89501
800-648-4882

Foothills Express
3377 N. Rainbow Boulevard
Las Vegas, Nevada 89130
702-878-2281

Fort Mojave Casino
Laughlin, Nevada 89028
702-535-5555

Forty-Niner (49er) Club
1241 N. Boulder Highway
Searchlight, Nevada 89046
702-297-1479

Forty-Niner (49er) Saloon & Casino
1556 N. Eastern Avenue
Las Vegas, Nevada 89101
702-649-2421

Four Jacks Hotel & Casino
Highway 93
Jackpot, Nevada 89825
702-755-2491

Four Queens Hotel & Casino
202 Fremont Street
Las Vegas, Nevada 89101
800-634-6045

Fourway Bar/Cafe/Casino
Highway 93 & I-80
Wells, Nevada 89835
702-752-3344

Friendly Fergie's Casino & Saloon
2430 S. Las Vegas Boulevard
Las Vegas, Nevada 89104
702-598-1985

Frontier Hotel & Gambling Hall
3120 S Las Vegas Boulevard
Las Vegas, Nevada 89109
800-421-7806

Gambler
211 N. Virginia Street
Reno, Nevada 89502
702-322-7620

The Gambler
1324 Victorian Avenue
Sparks, Nevada 89431
702-322-7620

Giudici's B Street Gambling Hall
1324 Victorian Avenue
Sparks, Nevada 89431
702-359-8868

Gloria's ll
1966 N. Rainbow Boulevard
Las Vegas, Nevada 89108
702-647-0744

Gold Coast Hotel & Casino
4000 W. Flamingo Road
Las Vegas, Nevada 89103
800-331-5334

Gold Country Motor Inn
2050 Idaho Street
Elko, Nevada 89801
702-738-8421

Gold Dust West Casino
444 Vine Street
Reno, Nevada 89503
702-323-2211

Gold'N Silver Inn
790 W. 4th Street
Reno, Nevada 89503
702-323-2696˙

Gold Ranch
Verdi, Nevada 89439
702-345-0556

Gold Spike Hotel & Casino
400 E. Ogden
Las Vegas, Nevada 89101
800-634-6703

Gold Strike Hotel & Gambling Hall
1 Main Street
Jean, Nevada 89019
800-634-1359

Gold Strike Inn & Casino
Highway 93 & Highway 466
Boulder City, Nevada 89005
702-293-5000

Golden Gate Hotel & Casino
1 Femont Street
Las Vegas, Nevada 89101
800-426-1906

Golden Nugget Hotel & Casino
129 E. Fremontl Street
Las Vegas, Nevada 89101
800-634-3403

Golden Nugget Hotel & Casino
2300 S. Casino Drive
Laughlin, Nevada 89029
800-955-7568

Hacienda Resort Hotel & Casino
3950 S. Las Vegas Boulevard
Las Vegas, Nevada 89119
800-634-6713

Hard Rock Hotel & Casino
4455 Paradise Road
Las Vegas, Nevada 89109
702-693-5000

Harrah's Casino Hotel
Highway 50 at State Line
Stateline, Nevada 89449
800-427-7247

Harrah's Casino Hotel
3473 S. Las Vegas Boulevard
Las Vegas, Nevada 89109
800-634-6765

Harrah's Casino Hotel
2900 S. Casino Drive
Laughlin, Nevada 89029
800-427-7247

Harrah's Casino Hotel
219 N. Center Street
Reno, Nevada 89501
800-648-3773

Harvey's Resort Hotel & Casino
Highway 50 at State Line
Stateline, Nevada 89449
800-553-1022

Headquarter's Bar & Casino
1345 S. Main Street
Fallon, Nevada 89406
702-423-6355

Hobey's Casino
5195 Sun Valley Drive
Sun Valley, Nevada 89443
702-673-0683

Holiday Hotel Casino
111 Mill Street
Reno, Nevada 89501
800-648-5431

Holiday Inn
3015 Idaho Street
Elko, Nevada 89801
702-738-8425

Holy Cow! Casino/Cafe/Brewery
3025 Sheridan Street
Las Vegas, Nevada 89041
702-732-2597

Horse Shu Club
Highway 93
Jackpot, Nevada 89825
702-755-7777

Horseshoe Casino
229 N. Virginia Street
Reno, Nevada 89501
702-323-7900

Hotel Nevada & Gambling Hall
501 Aultman Street
Ely, Nevada 89301
702-289-6665

Hotel San Remo Casino & Resort
115 E. Tropicana Avenue
Las Vegas, Nevada 89109
800-522-REMO

Howard Johnson Hotel & Casino
3111 W. Tropicana Avenue
Las Vegas, Nevada 89103
800-654-2000

Hyatt Regency Lake Tahoe
Resort & Casino
111 Country Club Drive
Incline Village, Nevada 89450
800-327-3910

Imperial Palace Hotel & Casino
3535 S. Las Vegas Boulevard
Las Vegas, Nevada 89109
702-731-3311

Indian Springs Hotel & Casino
Highway 95
Indian Springs, Nevada 89018
702-384-7449

Jackie Gaughan's Plaza Hotel & Casino
1 Main Street
Las Vegas, Nevada 89010
800-634-6575

Jackpot Owl Club Casino/Rest./Hotel
72 E. Front Street
Battle Mountain, Nevada 89820
702-635-2444

Jailhouse Motel & Casino
211 5th Street
Ely, Nevada 89301
800-841-5430

Jax Casino
485 Cornell Avenue
Lovelock, Nevada 89419
702-272-2288

Jerry's Nugget
1821 N. Las Vegas Boulevard
North Las Vegas, Nevada 89030
702-399-3000

Jim Kelly's Nugget
Crystal Bay, Nevada 89402
702-831-0455

JJ's Sierra Gambling Hall & Saloon
4350 N. Las Vegas Boulevard
Las Vegas, Nevada 89115
702-643-1955

Joe's Longhorn Casino
3016 E. Lake Mead Boulevard
North Las Vegas, Nevada 89030
702-642-1940

Joe's Tavern
537 Sierra Way
Hawthorne, Nevada 89415
702-945-2302

John Ascuaga's Nugget
1100 Nugget Avenue
Sparks, Nevada 89431
800-648-1177

Joker's Wild
920 Boulder Highway
Henderson, Nevada 89015
702-564-8100

Kactus Kate's Casino
I-15
Jean, Nevada 89019
702-477-5000

Keystone Club
Highway 351
Gabbs, Nevada 89409
702-285-4031

King 8 Hotel & Gambling Hall
3330 W. Tropicana Avenue
Las Vegas, Nevada 89103
702-736-8988

Klondike Inn & Casino
5191 S. Las Vegas Boulevard
Las Vegas, Nevada 89119
702-739-9351

Lady Luck Casino
206 N. 3rd Street
Las Vegas, Nevada 89101
800-634-6580

Lake Meade Lounge & Casino
846 E. Lake Mead Boulevard
Henderson, Nevada 89015
702-565-0297

Lake Tahoe Horizon Casino Resort
Highway 50 at State Line
Stateline, Nevada 89449
800-648-3322

Lakeside Inn & Casino
Highway 50
Lake Tahoe, Nevada 89449
800-624-7980

Las Vegas Club Hotel & Casino
Main & Fremont
Las Vegas, Nevada 89101
800-634-6532

Las Vegas Hilton Hotel & Casino
3000 Paradise Road
Las Vegas, Nevada 89109
800-732-7117

LeRoy's Horse & Sports Palace
114 S. 1st Street
Las Vegas, Nevada 89101

Ligouri's Bar & Casino
1133 N. Boulder Highway
Henderson, Nevada 89101

Longhorn Casino
5388 Boulder Highway
Las Vegas, Nevada 89101
702-435-9170

Loose Caboose Salon
15 N. Nellis Boulevard
Las Vegas, Nevada 89110
702-452-4500

Lucky Club
45 N. Main Street
Yerington, Nevada 89477
702-463-2868

Lucky Strike Mining Company Casino
642 S. Boulder Highway
Henderson, Nevada 89015
702-564-7118

Luxor Hotel & Casino
3900 S. Las Vegas Boulevard
Las Vegas, Nevada 89119
800-288-1000

Mac's Casino/Nevada Crossing Hotel
1045 Wendover Boulevard
W. Wendover, Nevada 89883
800-537-0207

Mad Matty's Bar/Casino/Grill
8100 W. Sahara Avenue
Las Vegas, Nevada 89117
702-254-9997

Mark Twain Saloon
62 South C Street
Virginia City, Nevada 89440
702-847-0599

Maxim Hotel & Casino
160 E. Flamingo Road
Las Vegas, Nevada 89109
702-731-4300

MGM Grand Hotel/Casino/Theme Park
3799 S. Las Vegas Boulevard
Las Vegas, Nevada 89109
800-929-1111

Mint Casino
1130 B Street
Sparks, Nevada 89421
702-359-4944

The Mirage
3400 S. Las Vegas Boulevard
Las Vegas, Nevada 89109
800-627-6667

Mizpah Casino
4300 Boulder Highway
Las Vegas, Nevada 89121
702-323-5194

Mizpah Hotel & Casino
100 Main Street
Tonopah, Nevada 89049
702-482-6202

Model T Casino & Hotel
1130 W. Winnemucca Boulevard
Winnemucca, Nevada 89445
702-623-2588

Monte Carlo Casino
1010 E. 6th Street
Reno, Nevada 89512
702-323-4183

Moulin Rouge Hotel & Casino
900 W. Bonanza Road
Las Vegas, Nevada 89106
702-648-5040

Mr. B's Casino
6000 E. I-80 Frontage Road
Mill City, Nevada 89418
702-538-7306

Mr. B's Casino
Ryepatch, Nevada 89419
702-538-7318

Mugshots Eatery & Casino
1120 N. Boulder Highway
Henderson, Nevada 89015
702-566-6577

Nevada Club Casino
224 N. Virginia Street
Reno, Nevada 89505
800-648-5022

Nevada Hotel Casino
36 E. Front Street
Battle Mountain, Nevada 89820
702-635-2453

Nevada Palace Hotel & Casino
5255 Boulder Highway
Las Vegas, Nevada 89122
800-634-6283

The Nugget
233 N. Virginia Street
Reno, Nevada 89501
702-323-0716

Old Reno Casino
44 W. Commercial Row
Reno, Nevada 89505
702-322-6971

Old West Inn Lounge & Casino
456 6th Street
Wells, Nevada 89835
702-752-3888

One-Eyed Jacks
4380 Boulder Highway
Las Vegas, Nevada 89121
702-434-9777

Opera House Saloon & Casino
2542 N. Las Vegas Boulevard
North Las Vegas, Nevada 89030
702-649-8801

Owl Club Casino & Motel
72 E. Front Street
Battle Mountain, Nevada 89820
702-635-5155

Owl Club & Steak House
Highway 50 at Main Street
Eureka, Nevada 89316
702-237-5280

P.J.Russo's
2300 S. Maryland Parkway
Las V egas, Nevada 89104
702-735-5454

P.T.' s Pub
347 North Nellis
Las Vegas, Nevada 89110
702-646-6657

P.T.'s Slsot Casino
44 Water Street
Henderson, Nevada 89105
702-564-4994

Palace Station Hotel & Casino
2411 W. Sahara Avenue
Las Vegas, Nevada 89102
800-634-3101

Peanut House Saloon
2292 S. Carson Stret
Carson City, Nevada 89701
702-882-8252

Peppermill Coffee Shop & Lounge
2985 S. Las Vegas Boulevard
Las Vegas, Nevada 89109
702-735-7635

Peppermill Inn & Casino
I-80
Wendover, Nevada 89883
800-648-9660

Petrelli's Fireside Inn & Casino
Ely, Nevada 89301
702-289-3765

Pioneer Hotel & Gambling Hall
2200 S. Casino Drive
Laughlin, Nevada 89029
800-634-3469

Pioneer Inn Casino
221 S. Virginia Street
Reno, Nevada 89501
800-879-8879

Plantation Station Gambling Hall
2121 Victorian Avenue
Sparks, Nevada 89431
702-359-9440

Player's Island Resort Casino Spa
930 W. Mesquite Boulevard
Mesquite, Nevada 89024
800-896-4567

Poker Palace Casino
2757 N. Las Vegas Boulevard
North Las Vegas, Nevada 89030
702-649-3799

Polar Palace Casino
2757 N. Las Vegas Boulevard
North Las Vegas, Nevada 89010
702-649-3799

Ponderosa Club & Arcade
Virginia City, Nevada 89440
702-847-0757

Popo's Gambling Hall
2501 E. Lake Mead Boulevard
North Las Vegas, Nevada 89030
702-649-8022

Port Tack Restaurant
3190 W. Sahara Avenue
Las Vegas, Nevada 89102
702-873-3345

Primadonna Resort & Casino
I-15
Jean, Nevada 89019
800-367-7383

Quality Inn & Casino
377 E. Flamingo Road
Las Vegas, Nevada 89109
702-733-7777

Queen of Hearts Hotel & Casino
19 E. Lewis Street
Las Vegas, Nevada 89101
702-382-8878

R-Bar
6000 W. Charleston Boulevard
Las Vegas, Nevada 89102
702-259-0120

Railroad Pass Hotel & Casino
2800 S. Boulder Highway
Henderson, Nevada 89015
800-654-0877

Rainbow Club & Casino
122 S. Water Street
Henderson, Nevada 89015
702-565-9777

Rainbow Vegas Hotel & Casino
401 S. Casino Center Boulevard
Las Vegas, Nevada 89101
800-634-6635

Ramada Express Hotel & Casino
2121 S. Casino Drive
Laughlin, Nevada 89028
800-272-6232

Red Garter Saloon & Gambling Hall
80 South C Street
Virginia City, Nevada 89440
702-874-0665

Red Lion Inn & Casino
741 W. Winnemucca Boulevard
Winnemucca, Nevada 89445
800-633-6435

Red Lion Inn & Casino
2065 Idaho Street
Elko, Nevada 89801
800-545-0044

Regency Casino
Laughlin, Nevada 89029
702-298-2439

Renata's Supper Club
4451 E. Sunset Road
Henderson, Nevada 89014
702-435-4000

Reno Hilton Resort
2500 East 2nd Street
Reno, Nevada 89595
702-789-2000

Reno Turf Club
Reno, Nevada 89505
702-323-1046

Rio Suite Hotel & Casino
3700 W. Flamingo Road
Las Vegas, Nevada 89101
800-752-9746

Riverboat Hotel & Casino
34 Wests 2nd Street
Reno, Nevada 89501
800-888-5525

Riviera Hotel & Casino
2901 S. Las Vegas Boulevard
Las Vegas, Nevada 89109
800-634-3420

Royal Hotel Casino
99 Convention Center Drive
Las Vegas, Nevada 89109
800-634-6118

Royal Hotel & Casino
4380 Boulder Highway
Las Vegas, Nevada 89212
702-735-6117

Saddle West Resort Hotel & Casino
1220 South Highway 160
Pahrump, Nevada 89048
800-522-5953

Sahara Hotel & Casino
2535 S. Las Vegas Boulevard
Las Vegas, Nevada 89109
800-634-6666

Sahara Saloon & Liquor Store
3345 E. Sahara Avenue
Las Vegas, Nevada 89104

Sam Boyd's California Hotel/Casino/RV
Park
12 Ogden Avenue
Las Vegas, Nevada 89101
702-385-1222

Sam Boyd's Fremond Hotel & Casino
200 E. Fremont Street
Las Vegas, Nevada 89101
800-634-6460

Sam's Town Gold River
Hotel & Gambling Hall
Casino Drive
Laughlin, Nevada 89028
800-835-2129

Sam's Town Hotel & Gambling Hall
5111 Boulder Highway
Las Vegas, Nevada 89122
800-634-6371

Sands Hotel & Casino
3355 S. Las Vegas Boulevard
Las Vegas, Nevada 89109
800-446-4678

Sands Regency Hotel & Mr. C's
345 N Arlington Avenue
Reno, Nevada 89501
800-648-3553

Sante Fee Hotel & Casino
4949 N. Rancho Drive
Las Vegas, Nevada 89130
800-872-6823

Sassy Sally's
32 Fremont Street
Las Vegas, Nevada 89101
702-382-5777

Say When
McDermitt, Nevada 89421
702-532-8515

Searchlight Nugget Casino
100 North Highway 95
Searchlight, Nevada 89046
702-297-1201

Sharkey's Nugget
1440 Highway 395
Gardnerville, Nevada 89410
702-782-3133

Showboat Hotel & Casino
2800 Fremont Street
Las Vegas, Nevada 89104
800-634-3484

Si Redd's Oasis
897 Mesquite Boulevard
Mesquite, Nevada 89024
702-346-5232

Silver City Casino
3001 S. Las Vegas Boulevard
Las Vegas, Nevada 89109
702-732-4152

Silver Club Hotel Casino
1040 Victorian Square
Sparks, Nevada 89432
800-648-1137

Silver Dollar Saloon & Casino
4848 Idaho Street
Elko, Nevada 89801
702-738-2217

Silver Legacy Resort & Casino
407 N. Virginia Street
Reno, Nevada 89501
702-322-3933

Silver Queen Hotel & Casino
28 North C Street
Virginia City, Nevada 89440
702-847-0440

Silver Smith Casino Resort
100 Wendover Boulevard
West Wendover, Nevada 89883
800-648-9668

Silver Strike Casino
Tonopah, Nevada 89049
702-482-9490

Skinny Dugan's Pub
4127 jW. Charleston Boulevard
Las Vegas, Nevada 89102
702-877-0522

Skyline Restaurant & Casino
1741 N. Boulder Highway
Henderson, Nevada 89015
702-565-9116

Slots-A-Fun Casino
3890 S. Las Vegas Boulevard
Las Vegas, Nevada 89109
800-634-3450

Stage Door Casino
4000 S. Audrie Street
Las Vegas, Nevada 89109
702-733-0124

Stagecoach Hotel & Casino
Highway 95
Beatty, Nevada 89003
702-553-2419

Stardust Resort & Casino
3000 S. Las Vegas Boulevard
Las Vegas, Nevada 89109
800-824-6033

Starlite Bowl
1201 Stardust Street
Reno, Nevada 89503
702-747-3522

Stateline Casino, Inc.
490 Mesquite Boulevard
Mesquite, Nevada 89024
702-346-5752

Station House Casino
100 E Main
Tonopah, Nevada 89049
702-482-8762

Stockman's Bar/Restaurant/Casino
1604 W. Williams Avenue
Fallon, Nevada 89406
702-423-2117

Stockmen's Motor Hotel & Casino
340 Commercial Street
Elko, Nevada 89801
702-738-5141

Sturgeon's Log Cabin
1420 Cornell Street
Lovelock, Nevada 89419
702-273-2971

Sundance Casino
Winnemucca, Nevada 89445
702-623-3336

Sundowner Hotel & Casino
450 N. Arlington Avenue
Reno, Nevada 89503
800-648-5490

Tahoe Biltmore Lodge & Casino
Highway 28
Crystal Bay, Nevada 89402
800-245-8667

Tamarack Grill & Bar
13101 S. Virginia Street
Reno, Nevada 89511
702-853-4567

Tom's Sunset Casino
444 W. Sunset Road
Henderson, Nevada 89015
702-564-5551

Topaz Lodge & Casino
Highway 395
Topaz Lake, Nevada 89410
800-962-0732

Treasure Club Casino
1144 B Street
 Sparks, Nevada 89531
702-356-7177

Treasure Island Hotel & Casino
3300 S. Las Vegas Boulevard
Las Vegas, Nevada 89109
800-944-7444

Treasury Club
Reno, Nevada 89510
702-356-7177

Triple J Bingo Hall & Casino
725 S. Racetrack Road
Henderson, Nevada 89015
702-566-5555

Triple Play
1875 S. Decatur Boulevard
Las Vegas, Nevada 89102
702-364-0808

Tropicana Resort & Casino
3801 S. Las Vegas Boulevard
Las Vegas, Nevada 89109
800-634-4000

Truck Inn-7 Z's Motel
485 Truck Inn Way
Fernley, Nevada 89408
800-635-8785

Vacation Village Hotel & Casino
6711 S. Las Vegas Boulevard
Las Vegas, Nevada 89119
702-897-1700

Valley Inn Club
Mesquite, Nevada 89024
702-346-2955

Virgin River Hotel & Casino
915 Mesquite Boulevard
Mesquite, Nevada 89024
800-346-7721

Virginian Hotel & Casino
140 N. Virginia Street
Reno, Nevada 89501
800-874-5558

Wells Chinatown Casino
455 S. Humboldt Avenue
Wells, Nevada 89835
702-752-2101

Western Hotel & Casino
815 E. Nichols Boulevard
Sparks, Nevada 89432
800-648-1170

Westward Ho Hotel & Casino
2900 S. Las Vegas Boulevard
Las Vegas, Nevada 89109
800-634-6803

Whiskey Pete's Hotel & Casino
I-15
Jean, Nevada 89019
800-367-7383

Whisle Stop
2839 W. Sahara Avenue
Las Vegas, Nevada 89102
702-873-2086

Winner's Hotel & Casino
185 W. Winnemucca Boulevard
Winnemucca, Nevada 89445
800-648-4770

New Jersey
Bally's Park Place Casino
Hotel & Tower
Park Place & The Boardwalk
Atlantic City, New Jersey 08401
800-772-7777

Caesars Atlantic City
2100 Pacific Avenue
Atlantic City, New Jersey '08401
800-223-7277

Claridge Casino Hotel
Park Place & The Boardwalk
Atlantic City, New Jersey 08401
800-257-5277

Harrah's Casino Hotel
777 Harrah's Boulevard
Atlantic City, New Jersey 08401
800-242-7724

Merv Griffin's Resort Casino & Hotel
North Carolina & The Boardwalk
Atlantic City, New Jersey 08401
800-336-6378

Sands Hotel & Casino
Indiana Avenue & The Boardwalk
Atlantic City, New Jersey 08401
800-257-8580

Showboat Hotel & Casino
Delaware Avenue & The Boardwalk
Atlantic City, New Jersey 08401
800-621-0200

The Grand--A Bally's Casino Resort
Boston & Pacific Avenues
Atlantic City, New Jersey 08401
800-843-4726

TropWorld Casino &
Entertainment Resort
Brighton Avenue & The Boardwalk
Atlantic City, New Jersey 08401
800-843-8767

Trump Plaza Hotel & Casino
Mississippi Avenue & The Boardwalk
Atlantic City, New Jersey 08401
800-677-7787

Trump Taj Mahal Casino Resort
Mississippi Avenue & The Boardwalk
Atlantic City, New Jersey 08401
800-825-8786

Trump's Castle Casino Resort
Huron Avenue & Brigantine Boulevard
Atlantic City, New Jerseyi 08401
800-777-1177

New Mexico

Camel Rock Casino
Sante Fe, New Mexico 87501
800-462-2635

Casino Sandia
Albuquerque, New Mexico 87184
505-897-2173

Inn of the Mountain Gods Casino
Carrizzo Canyon
Mescalero, New Mexico 88340
800-545-9011

Isleta Gaming Palace Casino
11000 Broadway SE
Albuquerque, New Mexico 87105
800-460-5686

Jicarilla Inn Bingo
Dulce, New Mexico 87528
800-742-1938

Oh-Kay Casino & Bingo
San Juan Pueblo, New Mexico 87566
505-747-1668

Pojoaque Gaming, Inc.
Sante Fe, New Mexico 87501
800-455-3313

Santa Ana Star Casino
54 Jemez Canyon Dam Road
Bernalillo, New Mexico 87004
505-867-0000

Sky City Tribal Casino
Acomita, New Mexico 87034
505-552-6017

North Dakota

Big "O" Casino
512 Dakota Avenue
Wahpeton, North Dakota 58705
701-642-2407

Blue Wolf Casino
I-94 at University
Fargo, North Dakota 58102
701-232-2019

Borrowed Buck's Roadhouse
1201 Westrac Drive
Fargo, North Dakota 58103
701-232-7861

Brass Mint Casino/Lounge/Holiday Inn
3803 13th Avenue South
Fargo, North Dakota 58103
701-282-2700

Bun Lounge Casino
1708 State Mill Road
Grand Forks, North Dakota 58201
701-746-1290

Cactus Jack's Gold Rush Casino
3402 Interstate Boulevard
Fargo, North Dakota 58103
701-280-0400

Charlie Brown's Casino
44 Gateway Drive
Grand Forks, North Dakota 58201
701-772-7620

Cheers Restaurant Lounge
1309 North Broadway
Minot, North Dakota 58701
701-852-5795

Dakota Lounge
1014 South 12th Street
Bismarck, North Dakota 58504
701-223-3514

Dakotah Sioux Casino
Tokio, North Dakota 58379
701-294-2109

Dakotah Sioux Casino
St. Michael, North Dakota 58370
701-766-4612

Doublewood Inn Casino Lounge
3333 13th Avenue South
Fargo, North Dakota 58103
701-235-3333

Doublewood Ramada Inn Casino
Exit 36 on I-94
Bismarck, North Dakota 58501
701-258-7000

El Rancho Motel Casino
1623 2nd Avenue West
Williston, North Dakota 58801
701-572-6321

El Roco
1730 13th Avenue North
Grand Forks, North Dakota 58201
701-772-8613

Flying J Travel
3150 39th Street
Fargo, North Dakota 58103
701-282-7766

Four Bears Casino & Lodge
Highway 23 West
New Town, North Dakota 58763
800-294-5454

Jailhouse Rock Casino
901 40th Street SW
Fargo, North Dakota 58103
800-543-9628

Nickels Lounge
800 South 3rd Street
Bismarck, North Dakota 58504
701-258-7700

Off-Broadway Lounge & Casino
605 E. Broadway Avenue
Bismarck, North Dakota 58501
701-255-6000

Penguin's Casino
2100 Burdick Expressway East
Minot, North Dakota 58701
701-839-0406

Perspectives Lounge & Casino
Radisson Hotel
201 5th Street North
Fargo, North Dakota 58102
800-333-3333

Pete's Lounge & Casino
710 First Avenue North
Grand Forks, North Dakota 59203
701-746-5411

Prairie Knights Casino & Lodge
Fort Yates, North Dakota 58538
800-425-8277

Ramada Inn Casino
1205 North 43rd Street
Grand Forks, North Dakota 58203
701-775-3951

Rick's Bar
2721 Main Avenue
Fargo, North Dakota 58103
701-232-8356

Sheraton Riverside Inn
2100 Burdick Expressway East
Minot, North Dakota 58701
701-852-2504

Silver Spur
501 Pleasant Avenue
Surry, North Dakota 58785
701-838-3616

Southgate Casino
2525 Washington Street South
Grand Forks, North Dakota 58203
701-775-6174

Stooge's Casino
10 3rd Street North
Grand Forks, North Dakota 58102
701-746-7189

Super-8 Lounge
2324 2nd Avenue
Williston, North Dakota 58801
701-572-8371

Turtle Mountain Chippewa Casino
Highway 5 West
Belcourt, North Dakota 58316
800-477-3497

Upper Deck Casino
707 28th Avenue North
Fargo, North Dakota 58102
701-235-1171

West End Casino
4220 5th Avenue North
Grand Forks, North Dakota 58203
701-775-9775

South Dakota

76 Motel & Restaurant
68 Main Street
Deadwood, South Dakota 57732
605-578-3476

Agency Bingo & Casino
Veterans Memorial Drive
Agency Village, South Dakota 5726
800-542-2876

B.B. Cody's
681 Main Street
Deadwood, South Dakota 57732
605-578-3430

Best Western Hickock House
137 Charles Strreet
Deadwood, South Dakota 57732
800-873-8174

Big Jake's Card Room
639 Main Street
Deadwood, South Dakota 57732
605-578-3631

Blackjack
270 Main Street
Deadwood, South Dakota 57732
605-578-9777

Bodega Bar & Cafe
662 Main Street
Deadwood, South Dakota 57732
605-578-1996

Buffalo Saloon
658 Main Street
Deadwood, South Dakota 57732
605-578-9993

Bullock Hotel & Casino
633 Main Street
Deadwood, South Dakota 57732
800-336-1876

Carnival Queen
606 Main Street
Deadwood, South Dakota 57732
605-578-1574

Carrie Nation Temperance Saloon
605 Main Street
Deadwood, South Dakota 57732
605-578-2036

Casey's
557 Main Street
Deadwood, South Dakota 57732
605-578-1105

DakotaTerritory Saloon
652 Main Street
Deadwood, South Dakota 57732
605-578-3566

Dakotah Sioux Casino
Sioux Valley Road
Watertown, South Dakota 57201
800-658-4717

Days Inn Casino
68 Main Street
Deadwood, South Dakota 57732
800-526-8277

Deadwood Dick's Saloon
5155 Sherman Street
Deadwood, South Dakota 57732

Deadwood Gulch Resort
10 Timm Lane
Deadwood, South Dakota 57732
800-695-1876

Deadwood Gulch Saloon
560 Main Street
Deadwood, Souith Dakota 57732
605-578-1207

Deadwood Livery
605 Main Street
Deadwood, South Dakota 57732
605-578-2036

Decker's Food Center Gaming
124 Sherman Street
Deadwood, South Dakota 57732
605-578-2722

Durty Nelly's
700 Main Street
Deadwood, South Dakota 57732
605-578-2241

Fairmont Hotel/Oyster Bay
626-628 Main Street
Deadwood, South Dakota 57732
605-578-2205

First Gold Hotel Gaming & Restaurant
270 Main Street
Deadwood, South Dakota 57732
800-274-1876

Fort Randall Casino Hotel
Wagner, South Dakota 57380
605-487-7871

Four Aces
531 Main Street
Deadwood, South Dakota 57732
605-578-2323

Fraternal Order of Eagles
409 Cliff Street
Deadwood, South Dakota 57732
605-578-1064

French Quarter
680 Main Street
Deadwood, South Dakota 57732
605-578-2100

Gold Coin Casino
21 Deadwood Street
Deadwood, South Dakota 57732
605-578-7701

Gold Dust Gaming &
Entertainment Complex
688 Main Street
Deadwood, South Dakota 57732
800-456-0533

Gold Nugget Inn/Diner/Casino
801 Main Street
Deadwood, South Dakota 57732
800-287-1251

Goldberg Gaming
670 Main Street
Deadwood, South Dakota 57732
605-578-1515

Golden Buffalo Casino
Lower Brule, South Dakota 57548
800-658-4554

Goldigger's Hotel & Gaming Estab.
629 Main Street
Deadwood, South Dakota 57732
800-456-2023

Grand River Casino
Mobridge, South Dakota 57601
800-475-3321

Hickock's Saloon
685 Main Street
Deadwood, South Dakota 57732
605-578-2222

Historic Franklin Hotel
700 Main Street
Deadwood, South Dakota 57732
800-688-1876

Jackpot Charlie's/Green Door Club
616 Main Street
Deadwood, South Dakota 57732
605-578-2014

Lady Luck
660 Main Street
Deadwood, South Dakota 57732
605-578-1162

Lariat Motel
360 Main Street
Deadwood, South Dakota 57732
605-578-1500

Legends
678 Main Street
Deadwood, South Dakota 57732
605-578-3141

Lillie's
671 Main Street
Deadwood, South Dakota 57732
605-578-3104

Lode Star Casino
Fort Thompson, South Dakota 57339
605-245-6000

Lucky-8 Casino & Super-8 Motel
196 Cliff
Deadwood, South Dakota 57732
605-578-2535

Lucky Miner
651 Main Street
Deadwood, South Dakota 57732
605-578-3363

Lucky Wrangler
638 Main Street
Deadwood, South Dakota 57732
605-578-3260

Midnight Star Gaming Emporium
677 Main Street
Deadwood, South Dakota 57732
800-999-6482

Mineral Palace Hotel & Gaming Complex
607 Main Street
Deadwood, South Dakota 57732
605-578-2036

Miss Kitty's/Chinatown Cafe
556 Main Street
Deadwood, South Dakota 57732
605-578-1715

Mustang
556 Main Street
Deadwood, South Dakota 57732
605-578-1715

Old Style Saloon #10
657 Main Street
Deadwood, South Dakota 57732
800-952-9398

Painted Pony Gaming
692 Main Street
Deadwood, South Dakota 57732
605-578-1012

Peacock Club
634 Main Street
Deadwood, South Dakota 57732
605-578-2025

Pink Palace
673 Main Street
Deadwood, South Dakota 57732
605-578-1276

Prairie Wind Casino
Pine Ridge, South Dakota 57770
605-535-6300

Rosebud Casino
Mission, South Dakota 57555
605-378-3800

Royal River Casino
Veterans Street
Flandreau, South Dakota 57028
800-833-8666

Shedd Jewelers
674 Main Street
Deadwood, South Dakota 57732
605-578-2494

Silver Dollar
686 Main Street
Deadwood, South Dakota 57732
605-578-2100

Silverado
709 Main Street
Deadwood, South Dakota 57732
605-578-3670

Slots of Luck
668 Main Street
Deadwood, South Dakota 57732
605-578-1979

Star of the West Casino
700 Main Street
Deadwood, South Dakota 57732
800-688-1876

The Depot & Mother Lode
Gaming Saloon
155 Sherman Street
Deadwood, South Dakota 57732
605-578-2699

Thunder Cove
Highway 85 South
Deadwood, South Dakota 57732
605-578-3045

Tin Lizzie Gamblling Hall
555 Main Street
Deadwood, South Dakota 57732
800-643-4490

Veterans of Foreign Wars
10 Pine Street
Deadwood, South Dakota 57732
605-578-9914

Will Bill's Bar & Gambling Hall
608 Main Street
Deadwood, South Dakota 57732
800-873-1876

Washington
Colville Tribal Bingo/
Okanogan Bingo Casino
41 Apple Way Road
Okanogan, Washington 98840
800-559-4643

Double Eagle Casino
Chewlah, Washington 99109
509-935-4406

Lummi Casino
2559 Lummi View Drive
Bellingham, Washington 98826
800-776-1337

Mill Bill Casino
455 East Wapato Lake Road
Manson, Washington 98831
509-687-2102

Muckleshoot Indian Casino
2402 Auburn Way South
Auburn, Washington 98002
206-804-4444

Nooksack River Casino
5048 Mt. Baker Highway
Deming, Washington 98244
800-223-2573

Quileute Tribe Casino
LaPush, Washington 98350
206-374-6739

Seven Cedars Casino
27056 Highway 101
Sequim, Washington 98382
800-458-2597

Spokane Tribal Indian Bingo & Casino
Smith Road
Chewelah, Washington 99109
509-935-6167

Swinomish Casino & Bingo
837 Casino Drive
Anacortes, Washington 98221
800-877-7529

Tulalip Bingo & Casino
6410 33rd Avenue NE
Marysville, Washington 98271
360-651-1111

Two Rivers Casino
6428B Highway 25 South
Davenport, Washington 99122
509-722-4000

Wisconsin

Bad River Bingo & Casino
Odanah, Wisconsin 54861
715-682-7121

Ho-Chunk Casino
Highway 12
Baraboo, Wisconsin 53913
800-746-2486

Hole-In-The-Wall Casino & Hotel
Highway 77 and Highway 35
Danbury, Wisconsin 54830
800-238-8946

Isle Vista Casino
Highway 13
Bayfield, Wisconsin 54814
800-226-8478

Lake of the Torches Casino
562 Peace Pipe Road
Lac Du Flambeau, Wisconsin 54538
800-258-6724

LCO Casino
Highways B & K
Hayward, Wisconsin 54843
800-422-2175

Majestic Pines Casino
Highway 54
Black River Falls, Wisconsin 54615
800-657-4621

Menominee Casino
Highway 47 & 55
Keshena, Wisconsin 54135
800-343-7778

Mohican North Star Casino & Bingo
W12180A County Road A
Bowler, Wisconsin 54416
800-952-0195

Mole Lake Casino
Highway 55
Crandon, Wisconsin 54520
800-236-9466

Oneida Bingo & Casino
2020 Airport Drive
Green Bay, Wisconsin 54313
800-236-4263

Potawatomi Bingo Casino
1721 W. Canal Street
Milwaukee, Wisconsin 53233
800-729-7244

Potawatomi Bingo &
Northern Lights Casino
Highway 32
Wabeno, Wisconsin 54566
800-487-9522

Rainbow Casino
949 County Trunk G
Nekoosa, Wisconsin 54457
800-782-4560

St. Croix Casino & Hotel
777 Highway 8
Turtle Lake, Wisconsin 54889
800-846-8946

Canada
Bear Claw Casino
White Bear Golf Course
Kenosee Lake, Sk. S0C 2S0
306-577-2313

Billy Barker Inn & Royal Casino
308 MacLean Street
Quesnel, BC V2J 2N9
604-992-7763

Buffalo Buck Casino
1800 Elphinstone
Regina, SK S4P 2Z6
306-781-9275

Cash Casino
4040 Blackfoot Tri SE
Calgary, AB T2G 4E6
403-287-1635

Casino ABS
1251 3rd Avenue South
Lethbridge, AB T1J 0K8
800-661-1375

Casino ABS
10549 102 Street
Edmonton, AB T5H 4K6
403-424-9467

Casino ABS South
7055 Argyll Road
Edmonton, AB T6C 4A5
403-463-9467

Casino de Charlevoix
183 Avenue Richelieu
Pointe-au-Pic, QB G0T 1M0
800-965-5355

Casino de Montreal
1 Avenue de Casino
Montreal, QB H3C 4W7
800-665-2274

Casino Windsor
445 Riverside Drive East
Windsor, ON N9A 6S1
800-991-7777

Club Regent
1425 Regent Avenue West
Winnipeg, MB R2C 3B2
204-957-2700

Crystal Casino
222 Broadway
Winnipeg, MB R3C 0R3
204-957-2600

Diamond Tooth Gertie's Gambling Hall
4th & Queen Streets
Dawson City, YK Y0B 1G0
403-993-5575

Digger's Territorial Casino
Highways 16 & 40
North Battleford, SK S9A 2Y9
306-445-2024

Eagles Nest Gaming Palace
Woodstock, NB E0J 2B0
800-447-0711

Emerald Casino
Saskatoon, SK S7K 4E4
403-460-1962

Gold Dust Casino
24 Boudreau Road
St. Albert, AB T8N 6R3
403-460-1962

Gold Rush Casino
South Saskatoon Highway
Prince Albert, SK S6V 5T1
306-764-1711

Golden Chance Casino
9423 79th Avenue
Grande Prarie, AB T8V 3A7
403-532-5330

Golden Nugget Casino
Main Street
Moose Jaw, SK S6H 4R3
306-692-2723

Grand Casino
725 SE Marine Drive
Vancouver, BC V5H 4H2
604-437-1696

Great Canadian Casino
8440 Bridgeport Road
Richmond, BC V6X 3C7
604-273-1895

Great Canadian Casino
15330 102A Avenue
Surrey, BC V3R 7R6
604-581-8915

Great Canadian Casino
1133 W. Hastings
Vancouver, BC V6E 3T3
604-268-1000

Great Canadian Casino
2477 Heather Street
Vancouver, BC V5Z 3Y2
604-872-5543

Great Canadian Casino
115 Chapel Street
Nanaimo, BC V9R 5H3

McPhilips Street Station
484 McPhilips Street
Winnipeg, MB R2X 2G8
204-957-2700

Palace Casino
8770 170th Street
Edmonton, AB T5T 4M2
403-444-2112

Prince George Casino
44 George Street
Prince George, BC V2L 1R6
604-561-2421

River Parks Casino
1919 Macleod Trail
Calgary, AB T2G 4S1
403-266-4355

Sheraton Casino
1969 Upper Water Street
Halifax, NS B3J 3R7
902-425-7777

Stampede Casino
Exhibition & Stampede Grounds
Calgary, AB T2P 2K8
800-661-1260

Triple C Casino
457 11th Street SE
Medicine Hat, AB T1A 1S9
403-526-6569

Wager's Casino
444 George Street
Prince George, BC V2L 1R6
604-561-2421

Winner Circle Casino
287 Wolverine Drive
Fort McMurray, AB T9H 4M3
403-743-5826

M840-TN